GERMAN INSIGNIA OF
WORLD WAR II

GERMAN INSIGNIA OF
WORLD WAR II

Edited by Chris Bishop and Adam Warner

CHARTWELL
BOOKS, INC.

This edition published in 2013 by
Chartwell Books, Inc.
A division of Book Sales, Inc.
276 Fifth Avenue Suite 206
New York, New York 10001
USA

ISBN-13: 978-0-7858-3034-4

Published by
Amber Books Ltd
74–77 White Lion Street
London
N1 9PF
United Kingdom
www.amberbooks.co.uk
Appstore: itunes.com/apps/amberbooksltd
Facebook: www.facebook.com/amberbooks
Twitter: @amberbooks

This material was previously published as part of the reference set *Hitler's Third Reich*.

Contributors: Chris Bishop, Kurt Steiner, Adam Warner, William Wilson
The publisher would like to thank Ulric of England (PO Box 55, Church Stretton, Shropshire SY6 6WR) for allowing photography of his extensive collection
Illustrators: Peter Harper, Chris Bishop
Picture credits: Aerospace, AKG, Bundesarchiv, John Weal, Popperfoto, Robert Hunt Library, Topham, US Holocaust Memorial Museum

Printed in China

CONTENTS

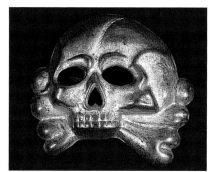

DEATH'S HEAD

The piratical skull and crossbones or *Totenkopf* has become infamous as a symbol of the SS. But for Germans, the Death's Head has a much older history, rich in military associations.

Left: Kurt 'Panzer' Mayer was the youngest divisional commander in the SS. Seen here as a Sturmbannführer on the Eastern Front, he is wearing an NCO-pattern 'crusher' field cap with an old Prussian-style Totenkopf.

Above: Right-wing Freikorps volunteers played a major part in the political unrest which followed Germany's defeat in World War I. A number of Freikorps units adopted the Death's head as a symbol.

DEATH'S HEADS were associated with the SS from the beginning of the Nazi period. The then-tiny formation which was Hitler's bodyguard wore them, to distinguish the chosen elite from the brawling mass of brownshirted SA stormtroopers. *Totenkopfs* adorned the smart uniforms of Hitler's *Leibstandarte-SS* guard during the party rallies of the 1930s, and were still being worn at the end of the war, as camouflaged Waffen SS soldiers made their last, futile defence of Berlin against the overwhelming might of the Red Army. But it was as the chosen symbol of the *Totenkopfverbande* – the concentration camp guards – that the Death's Head acquired its horrific associations.

MILITARY SIGNIFICANCE

However, the *Totenkopf* was not chosen for its ghoulish appearance: rather it was a way of linking the SS with famous military units of German history. As a symbol of mortality, the skull and crossbones can be found on graves and headstones all over the world. It is also an ancient military symbol, since war is absolute and allows no half measures between defeat or victory. For the soldier, the Death's Head carries two messages – death or glory – and it consequently became the cap badge or insignia of élite formations which were prepared to fight to the death.

HISTORICAL SYMBOL

In the 18th century the Prussian *Leib-Husaren* – the royal bodyguard – adopted black uniforms with a large *Totenkopf* badge on their fur busbies, in memory of King Fredrick William I. The Deaths Head Hussars were among the Prussian forces which proved decisive on the field of Waterloo. Troops from Brunswick also wore their own version of the Deaths Head.

Left: The black SS peaked service cap or Schirmmütze was standard issue to all members of the SS in the mid- to late-1930s, though it was rarely worn after the outbreak of war. This is the NCO/other ranks version: officers wore a cap with braided chinstraps rather than the leather strap seen here.

Left: At the end of 1935 a grey-version of the Schirmmütze was introduced for members of the Leib-standarte and other armed SS units. It became general from 1939, as the black SS uniform ceased to be worn.

Left: Collar patches of an Hauptsturm-führer (Captain) of the 3rd SS Panzer Division Totenkopf. This was the only formation to use Death's Head collar patches: all other Waffen SS units had SS runes on their right collars.

TOTENKOPF OF THE SS

Above: Although many brave men fought under the Totenkopf, it also presided over some of the war's most shameful deeds – as when SS troops massacred more than 70 Americans at Malmédy.

During World War I a number of German army units used the *Totenkopf* as a symbol, notably the 1st and 2nd Battalions of Infantry Regiment 17 and the 2nd Battalion of Cavalry Regiment 13. In the last year of the war, Stormtroopers and flamethrower units also went into battle under the Death's Head, as did the first German tank units. As a result the Death's Head was to become the standard insignia of German armoured troops during World War II.

In the chaotic conditions prevailing in Germany at the end of World War I, a number of Freikorps units painted crude Death's Heads on their helmets and vehicles. The first Nazi unit to wear the symbol was the *Stosstrupp* Adolf Hitler, the leader's personal bodyguard established in 1923, which was to evolve into the SS. By using the *Totenkopf* they associated themselves not only with élite fighting units, but also with those they saw as holding the front line in the struggle against Bolshevism and Socialism.

WAR SURPLUS

Initially the SS used war surplus examples of the original Prussian pattern *Totenkopf*, and continued to do so until 1934 when the newly expanded German army established its first Panzer units. *Panzertruppen* wore a black uniform, pink edged collar patches and an aluminium Deaths Head in the Prussian pattern. It was then that the SS evolved its own variant, distinct from the traditional version used by the army. Other military units to sport Deaths Heads during World War II included the army 5th Cavalry Regiment, naval coast gunners in Danzig, and the Luftwaffe's Kampfgruppe 54.

Left: Sepp Dietrich rose through the SS from being a street thug to command an Army Group. He is seen here in winter gear, with a 1934-pattern Totenkopf on his fur hat.

When the *Stosstrupp Adolf Hitler* was formed in the mid-1920s as Hitler's body guard they adopted a black cap and distinctive insignia to set themselves apart from the brown ranks of the SA. The cap eagle held a *Totenkopf* in its claws rather than the red, black and white national cockade.

As the party expanded, the bodyguards provided the nucleus for a number of small protection squads which provided a party-wide security force. These *Schutzstaffeln* quickly became known as the SS.

Originally, the SS used the traditional Prussian pattern of Death's Head, but in 1934 a new design with a jaw bone was adopted to distinguish the SS version from those used by the Wehrmacht. This was initially made in coated bronze,

Below: The first Death's Heads used by the SS were originally manufactured during World War I for some of the toughest, hardest fighting units of the Kaiser's army. These included storm troopers, early tank crews, and flamethrower troops.

but later appeared in stamped aluminium, in zinc alloy, in cloth and and in woven aluminium thread for the 1943 pattern combat caps. The *Totenkopf* also appeared on the SS trumpet banners, on drum covers, on SS rings, on daggers and on flags.

As the SS expanded it split into two. The Waffen-SS fought as soldiers in Russia, Italy and north west Europe.

The Allgemeine or General SS was the home-based service, and included the sinister SS-*Totenkopfverbande* (SSTV) who provided the guards for concentration camps and later for extermination camps.

The SSTV provided much of the manpower for the *Totenkopf* field division which was formed in 1939. Whereas most of the Waffen-SS wore the SS runes on the right collar patch and their rank on the other, the men of the *Totenkopf* division wore the Death's Head on their collars and as a cuffband to show their different origin.

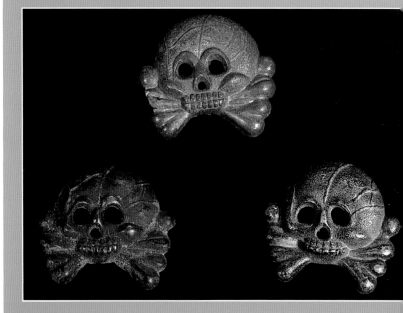

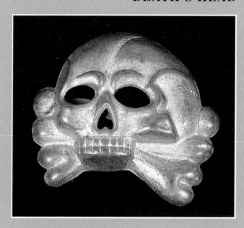

Right: The original Prussian-style Totenkopf was based on a jewelled Death's Head carried in the funeral procession of King Fredrick William I of Prussia, who died in 1740. The Totenkopf was adopted as a cap badge by the bodyguard of his son, Frederick the Great.

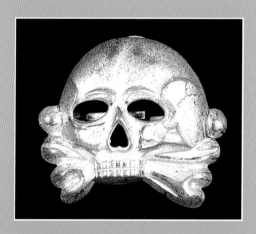

Right: The SS initially used World War I army surplus Totenkopf cap badges. As the organisation expanded, it needed new supplies. The Party ordered more from the Munich firm of Deschler, and many thousands were struck between 1923 and 1934.

Above: Cloth badges were sewn onto SS field caps. The original pattern featured separate Eagles and Death's Heads: these one piece badges was designed for Tyrolean-style peaked caps worn from 1943.

Below: SS equipment did not come through the Army's supply system: orders were placed by the Reichs-zeugmeisterei der NSDAP, the Nazi Party's contracts office. All such items were marked with the RZM stamp.

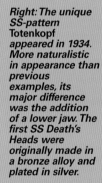

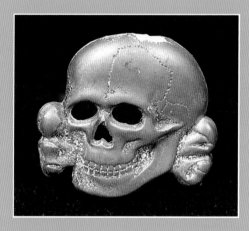

Right: The unique SS-pattern Totenkopf appeared in 1934. More naturalistic in appearance than previous examples, its major difference was the addition of a lower jaw. The first SS Death's Heads were originally made in a bronze alloy and plated in silver.

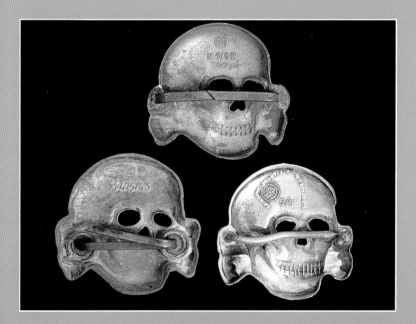

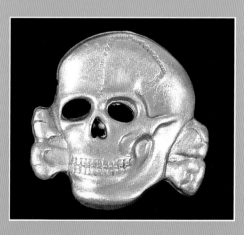

RIGHT: As the war progressed, luxuries like silver-plated cap badges went by the board, and the SS Totenkopf began to be made much more simply and cheaply. Late-war Death's Heads were stamped out of aluminium or zinc-based alloys.

ONE OF THE key images of the Nuremberg Rallies is of massed ranks of Storm Troopers, SS men and Nazi Party officials framed by hundreds of red, white and black swastika banners, the whole assembly echoing to the roar of thousands of voices shouting "Sieg Heil".

The other abiding image is of Adolf Hitler's sweating face glistening in the stage lighting, holding his listeners spellbound as he rants against Jews, Marxists, bolshevists, pacifists, the Treaty of Versailles, the Weimar Republic, France and Soviet Russia.

This image was created in large part by Leni Riefenstahl's powerful film *Triumph des Willens* ('The Triumph of the Will') which recorded the 1934 rally. However, it does not reflect the modest beginnings of the annual Nazi party gatherings.

The rallies were known as *Parteitage* or Party Days. The first was held in Munich in 1923 and attracted 20,000 spectators and party members. The SA (*Sturmabteilung* or assault detachment) was on call for a modest parade. Briefly known on its foundation in 1921 as the party's 'Gymnastics and Sports Division', the SA was the Nazi paramilitary wing, intended to provide the movement with an offensive street fighting force.

At the urging of Julius Streicher, the second rally, in August 1923, was held at Nuremberg. This included a two hour parade by 80,000 Storm Troopers and at the *Ausstellungshalle* (Exhibition Hall) Hitler gave the same speech four times to audiences of 2,000.

HITLER BANNED

For his part in the 1923 Beer Hall Putsch, Hitler served nine months of a five year sentence in Landsberg am Lech prison. Party membership was greatly reduced after the Putsch, and after his release Hitler was banned from political activity in most major cities, so the next rally in Weimar was not held until July 1926.

This was the first rally to be called a *Parteitag*. It began on

NUREMBERG RALLIES

Below: Adolf Hitler addresses more than a quarter of a million followers at the 1933 rally – the first after the Nazis came to power.

July 3 and ended at noon the following day. The *Blutfahne* ceremony was held in secret. Special committees were established to attract youth, labour and women to the Party, and the meeting marked the emergence of Dr Joseph Goebbels as a major personality.

The fourth rally, at Nuremberg in August 1927 was still quite a modest affair, though it lasted for three days. Hitler was now free from his political ban, and the *Blutfahne* ceremony was held in public. The highlight of this rally was a torchlight parade through the narrow medieval streets of the city. This rally saw another new name come to the fore with the prominent appearance of Heinrich Himmler.

PARTY SPECTACULAR

The depression saw Party membership on the rise again, and the rally between August 2 and 5, 1929 was the first truly spectacular event. The theme was 'composure'. All the major buildings in the city, including the *Kulturvereinhaus* (House of

The incredible spectaculars which took place at Nuremberg have gone down in history as the definitive pre-war face of the Third Reich.

Above: Hitler salutes the SA as they march past during the 1927 rally. This was the fourth such occasion, and was still a relatively modest affair – at least by the standards of Party Days to come.

Below inset: The first real party rally took place in Munich in January 1923, 11 months before the Nazi attempt to seize power. Highlight of the event was a parade by the paramilitary SA.

"...at Party Days, the marriage between the NSDAP and the people is consummated anew, year after year."

Culture) and the huge open spaces of the *Zeppelinwiese* and *Luitpoldhain* were used. More than 2,000 delegates assembled to hear speeches from Hitler, Goebbels and Streicher. There were athletes with burning torches, the formation of human swastikas and dazzling fireworks.

To celebrate Hitler's assumption of power, the rally in 1933 was called the 'Congress of Victory'. Numbers attending had increased still further, and the logistic effort to house and feed half a million Nazis required the requisitioning of churches, factories and public buildings as well as assembling tented villages with field kitchens.

"Swastika on our helmet, black-white-red armband, *Sturm abteilung* Hitler is our name"

Early SA Fighting Song

In May that year the successful young architect Albert Speer undertook the design work on a rally at Tempelhof Field in Berlin, and his use of massed flags and special lighting effects would become a feature of future rallies. Recognising his talent Hitler commissioned him in 1934 to design the party rally grounds at Nuremberg.

The 1934 rally at Nuremberg lasted from September 3 to 10. Former actress turned director

Left: Two thousand senior delegates gather in Nuremberg's Kulturvereinhaus to hear Hitler, Goebbels and others speak during the 1929 rally. After a period in isolation, party membership was again growing, and the annual party days were becoming more and more spectacular.

Consecration of the banners
Touched with the blood of martyrs: the *Blutfahne*

A KEY FEATURE of all Party Rallies was the appearance of the *Blutfahne*, or Blood Banner. Probably the most revered symbol in the Third Reich, the *Blutfahne* was one of the flags used during the abortive Munich Putsch of 1923. Carried by Heinrich Trambauer as the Nazis clashed with state police in Odeon Square, it was spattered with the blood of Andreas Bauriedl who was one of 16 men killed during the rising. Regarded as a holy relic, it was placed in the keeping of the SS in 1926, and Jakob Grimminger was appointed standard bearer. Grimminger was a veteran of both World War I and of street fights with the communists, and would remain in his position as standard bearer until the Blood Banner disappeared at the end of the war.

The *Blutfahne* was displayed at all major Nazi ceremonials, the most prominent of which was the 'consecration' of the Feldzeichen or banners of newly-formed SA units and SS *Standarten*. These almost invariably took place during the annual Nuremberg party rallies.

In a ritual which resembled the blessing of military colours in Christian armies, Hitler acted like a high-priest. Holding the Blood Banner in one hand and the new standard as the other, he acted as the medium by which the magic of one sacred symbol was transmitted to the other. By holding the two flags in contact for a few seconds, the *Blutfahne* made a 'mystic' connection between the new Nazi units and the fighters and martyrs of the early days of the movement.

This ritual would remain one of the most important of all the Nuremberg ceremonies, and would be extensively recorded on photographs and in film.

Above: The first four party Feldzeichen *or battlefield standards are paraded on Munich's Marsfeld in 1923.*

Left: Hitler consecrates new Feldzeichen *in a quasi-religious ceremony by touching them with the Blutfahne.*

Right: The Blutfahne *was in the keeping of the SS, and was carried till its disappearance at the end of the war by Jakob Grimminger.*

Below: The four original standards were the first of many: each represented a regiment-sized Standarte *of the SS or the SA.*

Above: From 1934 the Reich Labour Service played an important role at Nuremberg: this is the 'Army of Labour' on parade at the 1935 rally.

Right: Members of the Motorised SA pass through the ancient streets of Nuremberg. After the 1934 rally this organisation became the NSKK (National-sozialistische KraftfahrerKorps or Nazi motor corps)

Below: Although vastly outnumbered by the SA, the black-shirted SS was to become much more influential in National Socialist Germany.

Leni Riefenstahl deployed 30 cameramen and had special trackways and elevators built to produce dramatic shots of the rally. The film which emerged is probably the most powerful piece of propaganda ever created. It turned Hitler into a Wagnerian hero, arriving by aircraft through towering clouds. Riefenstahl's memorable images included massive torchlight processions, the unfurling of 21,000 flags and the sight of 50,000 men of the *Reichsarbietsdienst* standing with their shovels glittering in the sun. 'Triumph of the Will' received a National State Prize, the gold medal of the Venice Film Festival and a Grand Prix of the French government at the Paris Film Festival.

ANTISEMITIC LAWS

Hitler took the opportunity of the 1935 rally to present the Nuremberg Laws on race and citizenship. Directed primarily at the Jews, they made clear to the rest of the world the true character of the new German government. For the first time the armed forces paraded tanks, armoured cars and aircraft.

In 1936 in a rally with the theme 'Honour and Freedom' there were more military parades. A year later in a ranting speech Hitler told his audience that the Third Reich would "last for a thousand years".

The final and greatest Nuremberg rally was held from September 5 to 12, 1938. Each day was dedicated to a separate theme: Welcome, Congress of Labour, Fellowship, Politics, Youth, Storm Troopers, and finally the Armed Forces. The rally incorporated all the accumulated experience of past years with parades, banners, reviews, speeches, torchlight processions and fireworks. Over one million people attended and hundreds of reporters from throughout the world covered an event which seemed like a triumph, but was in reality the requiem for the Reich.

Left: Nuremberg was not the only site of major Nazi occasions: here Hitler addresses a political meeting at Brunswick during the Party's expansion in the years before coming to power.

Above: Hitler ascends the Bückeberg through tens of thousands of farming families. Shorn of all Christian symbolism, the annual Nazi harvest festival took place a month after the Parteitage.

Below: Hitler inspects the ceremonial guard drawn from the Leibstandarte Adolf Hitler, the elite SS formation which grew out of the Führer's original SS bodyguard squads of the 1920s.

SA STORM TROOPERS

The brown-shirted stormtroopers of the *Sturmabteilung*, or SA, were the shock troops of the National Socialist movement. Their task was to deal with enemies of the party – violently, if necessary.

T HE SA WAS THE paramilitary wing of the Nazi Party. Designed to operate in the rough and tumble that was Bavarian politics in the years after World War I, the members of the *Sturmabteilung* – Assault Detachment – were quite willing to trade hard knocks with political opponents.

As the party grew, so did the SA. By the time that Hitler came to power in 1933, it numbered more than two million men – 20 times the size of the regular army – and under the firebrand leadership of Ernst Röhm it was a potential threat to the Führer himself. But its days of influence were numbered: with the murderous 'Night of the Long Knives' in 1934, the organisation lost its direction and leadership. It was to continue through the war, but was never the force it had been.

EARLY DAYS

The origins of the SA date back to 1921. A fair proportion of the party membership were former soldiers. Most had been members of the right-wing *Freikorps* which fought leftists for control of the streets of Munich. Their only uniform was a crude

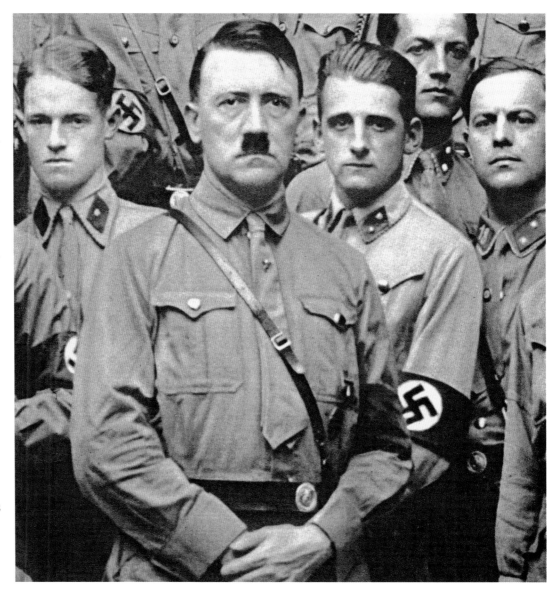

Kampfbinde, or swastika armband, worn on the left sleeve.

Hitler imposed some structure onto the party fighters, incorporating them into a single organisation. Originally called the 'Sports and Gymnastics Division' – paramilitary organisations were illegal in Germany under the terms of the Treaty of Versailles – they were soon renamed the SA.

The SA's task was to protect party meetings, disrupt the meetings of any opposing parties, and to march and look impressive at rallies. With the failure of the 1923 Putsch, the SA was declared illegal, but by the late 1920s it was again at the forefront of Nazi expansion.

The SA's increasing power under Ernst Röhm worried both the army and rival Nazis. After the 'Blood Purge' of 1934, which saw the SA leaders killed, power shifted to Himmler's SS.

German rearmament meant that much of the SA's strength was absorbed into the armed forces. The SA remained in existence, but its role had been reduced to providing basic pre-military training for young Germans.

Above: In the early days SA uniforms lacked consistency, members often wearing their old military uniforms, stripped of badges but with the addition of a red, white and black Swastika armband.

Left: Adolf Hitler stands surrounded by his faithful followers: young brownshirts attending the NSDAP's Führerschule, or leadership school. Most have the rank of Scharführer or Oberscharführer.

SA badges and insignia, clockwise from top left: an other-ranks kepi, an SA song book, a 1933 pattern dagger, a medical collar patch from the 7th Jägerstandarte, an SA belt, a commemorative badge from the 1931 Brunswick SA rally, an SA Kampfbinde (armband), a 1929 Nuremberg rally badge, and a Westphalian SA Sports badge (worn on the front of a sports singlet).

BROWN SHIRTS

*Above: SA Stabschef
Ernst Röhm works in his
palatial office. Röhm was
a former army officer
who in 10 years built the
SA up from a band of
street thugs to a two-
million-strong force with
ambitions to replace the
German army.*

*Right: Senior SA officers
march through the
streets of Nuremberg on
their way to a meeting.
By the 1930s the original
simple SA brownshirt
had evolved into a range
of uniform clothing for
all occasions.*

*Below: Once the Nazis
came to power, the SA
was unleashed on their
foes. Here a storm-
trooper stands guard
over communists,
arrested in a night raid.
Most will be sent to
concentration camps.*

The Brownshirt uniform
came into being in 1924.
Hitler, always alive to the
effects of propaganda and
always ready to make a
visual impact, was well
aware of the benefits of an
easily distinguished appearance. He had also seen how
effective Mussolini's Fascist
Blackshirts had been in Italy.

However, the choice of
brown shirts was more by
chance than by design.
Gerhard Rossbach was a
former *Freikorps* leader and
one of the most influential
of the early SA leaders. In
1924 he discovered a large
stock of surplus Imperial
Army tropical shirts, and
bought them for the
movement.

Once he had been
released from Landsberg
prison, Adolf Hitler decided
that these would be the
basis of the new SA
uniform, and ordered kepis,
ties, and breeches to
complete the ensemble.

In November 1926,
the SA began using
Kragenspiegel or collar
patches to denote rank (left
collar) and unit (right collar).
They were in the local State
colours, indicating which
region the unit came from:
black and white for Berlin,
red and white for Hamburg,
blue and white for Munich
and so on.

The collar patches also
carried specialist insignia.
These included those for
aviation units, as well as for
Jäger (light infantry), medical, pioneer, naval, and
mountain units.

Cuff titles were used
where units had been
honoured with the name of
a Nazi 'martyr'.

*Below: SA and SS service daggers, or Dienstdolch, were introduced
in 1933 by the SA's interim Chief of Staff, Obergruppenführer von
Krausser. Based on a Swiss-German dagger style dating back to the
16th century, the SA daggers were issued in huge numbers. Less
common were a number of special presentation versions. This is a
rare Röhm dagger, distributed in February 1934 to senior SS men by
SA Stabschef Ernst Röhm. Engraved on the blade is the inscription
In Herzlicher Kameradschaft, Ernst Röhm (In heartfelt comradeship,
Ernst Röhm). Five months later Röhm and the senior SA leadership
were dead, purged by the SS in the 'Night of the Long Knives', and
many of the recipients of the dagger had the inscription erased.*

Above: The SA stressed sports as an important part of training. Members of the SA and the NSDAP competed for the SA Sports Badge at official meetings, and officials wore the insignia of the SA Sports Badge Association.

Below: This tunic belonged to SA Obergruppenführer (General) Wilhelm Helfer. A World War I veteran, he took part in the 1923 Putsch, and was the 44th holder of the 'Blood Order', seen here on the right breast pocket. On the left pocket are the Black Wound Badge (left), War Merit Cross in Silver (bottom), 1931 Brunswick Rally Badge (right) and the NSDAP Gold Party Badge of Honour (top).

Above: The brownshirt worn by a scharführer (NCO) of Jägerstandarte 3 Dietrich Eckart. The metal gorget was worn by standard bearers. Named after one of the founders of the Nazi movement, the unit was given the title by Hitler in 1937

Below: Insignia of SA Standarten 137, based in Westphalia. The unit was named after Ludwig Knickmann, an early Nazi fighter. He died in 1923 during the Allied occupation of the Ruhr, drowning while trying to swim a river to escape from a Belgian patrol.

HITLER JUGEND

THE HITLER Youth was founded in 1926 by Kurt Gruber. A branch of the SA, it was originally known as the Youth League of the NSDAP, and its formation reflected the popularity of youth movements all over Europe in the 1920s and 1930s. It received official party recognition at the 1926 Reich Party Congress, and it was there that Julius Streicher coined the name *Hitlerjugend*, often abbreviated HJ.

In 1931, the 24-year-old Baldur von Schirach was appointed its leader, and in 1933 it absorbed all other youth movements in Germany. The only exceptions were a number of Catholic groups, which were banned in 1936. In April 1939, a *Jugenddienstverordnung* or 'Youth Service Order' made

From tiny beginnings in 1926, the Hitler Youth grew with the Nazi party to become the dominant organisation for German children and teenagers.

Below right: The Bund deutscher Mädel – League of German Girls – was the female equivalent to the Hitler Youth.

Right: One of the most evocative of all images of the Hitler Youth is that of a trumpeter sounding a fanfare at party occasions.

Below: The 'youth' days at the annual Nuremberg rallies were amongst the most enthusiastically attended of all. Youth was important to Hitler and the Nazis – if you catch them young and impressionable, you have a convert for life.

membership in the HJ
compulsory for all German
girls and boys. At its height, the
movement numbered more than
3.5 million members.

ENTRY INTO THE HJ

Initially, boys and girls aged
between 10 and 14 entered the
Jungvolk or *Jungmadel*. A boy
entering the *Jungvolk* was known
as a *Pimpf*, and had to pass an
entrance test which included
reciting the 'Horst Wessel' song
and running 50 metres in 12
seconds. Activities included two-
day cross-country hikes,
practising semaphore and
learning arms drill.

At 14, girls moved on to the
Bund Deutscher Mädel. Though
girls also undertook long
marches and went on camps, the
main emphasis of their training
was on domestic or farm work.
Suitably 'Nordic' girls from
Holland, Flanders, Norway and
Denmark were also eligible for
such *landdienst* or land service.

At 15, boys entered the HJ
proper. There they undertook
training that would prepare them

Above: The coloured band on the first pattern Hitler Jugend peaked cap matched the piping on the shoulder patches, and indicated the Bann or Oberbann to which the member belonged. The belt buckle carried the Hitler Youth motto – Blut und Ehre (Blood and Honour).

Below: A collection of certificates awarded to a Hitler Youth member very late in the war. The central piece is the Oath of Allegiance to the Führer, taken by every member of the Hitler Youth as he made the transition from the Deutsche Jungvolk at the age of 14.

for military service. They were taught to drive, to fly gliders, to handle small craft, to shoot, and were trained in small unit tactics.

With the outbreak of war older HJ members were drafted into fire fighting and air raid protection duties, freeing adults for military service. By the end of September 1939 more than a million *Hitlerjugend* were helping with the war effort. Most of the HJ leaders joined the fighting services – Baldur von Schirach entering the army's elite *Grossdeutschland* infantry regiment.

BOYS INTO BATTLE

From 1943, with the war turning against Germany, the HJ entered combat – primarily crewing anti-aircraft guns. However, the most radical move came when 17- and 18-year olds were given the opportunity to serve in the 12th SS Panzer Division *Hitlerjugend*. The division fought fanatically in Normandy, suffering 60% killed,

Above: Military training was a key part of the HJ's activities. The boys were introduced to it young: these are 11- and 12-year old pimpfs of the Jungvolk.

wounded or missing in under a month.

By the end of the war girls from the BdM were serving in Flak units, and some fought as anti-tank gunners outside Vienna. Others took part in the fierce but hopeless defence of Berlin against the Russians. Indeed, the Hitler Youth figured largely in the last occasion Hitler was seen in public. On April 20 1945 – the Führer's birthday – he emerged from the Führerbunker to present Iron Crosses to a group of 14-year-old HJ boys. Then he went back underground, never to see the light of day again.

Below: Any innocence which the Hitlerjugend may have had was lost in the fires of war. By the end of the conflict HJ members were manning anti-aircraft and anti-tank guns, fighting on all fronts.

CHILDREN OF THE REICH

The HJ and the BdM had their own distinctive uniforms and insignia. Girls wore short brown jackets, full-length black skirts, white blouses and neckerchiefs, white socks and black shoes. Boys wore brown shirts and shorts with black neckerchief and a black belt with cross strap.

The HJ swastika appeared inside a white diamond with red tips at top and bottom. On armbands this appeared on a white diamond, with a narrow white bar running through the centre of the red band. Epaulets and a triangular badge sewn onto the left sleeve indicated to which HJ region the wearer belonged. The lower sleeve also carried badges indicating skills and qualifications. Adult leaders wore a single-breasted, four-pocketed mustard-coloured tunic with black trousers and peaked cap. The swastika also appeared on the handle of an HJ member's most treasured possession, his dagger. The bayonet-style sheathe knife bore the motto *Blut und Ehre* – 'Blood and Honour'. With over 20,000,000 being manufactured, more Hitler Youth daggers were made than any other edged weapon of the Nazi period.

Below: The uniform of a Hitler Youth Gebietsführer (Regional Leader) from Bavaria. The extra gold piping under the triangular unit badge indicates a 'Tradition Unit', which had been in existence since before 1933. The two pocket insignia are the War Merit cross and the Golden Leader's Sports Badge, awarded annually for success in the Decathlon.

Above: The bayonet-style knife was very much a symbol of the Hitler Jugend. It had an immense symbolic and psychological significance – only specially selected adults were allowed to carry such weapons, whereas every member of the HJ was issued with one.

Below: The Hitler Youth used two patterns of shoulder straps. The first pattern, issued from around 1933 to 1938, had coloured piping indicating their Bann or unit and also carried rank insignia. Second pattern straps (1938-1945) were generally black, or dark blue for members of the Marine-HJ.

Below: The triangular patches worn by HJ members on their upper right sleeves usually showed the wearer's Obergebiet or main administrative district – Nord, Süd, Ost, West or Mitte. The second line referred to his Gebiet or home district. Children of German parentage living abroad were encouraged to join the HJ, and wore appropriate triangles. The special green Landjahr sleeve badge was worn by HJ members who had completed a year as a volunteer worker on the land. The 'S' rune on the right indicates that the wearer was a member of the Deutsche Jungvolk, the junior HJ.

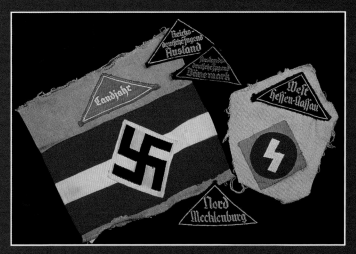

23

PARTY COLOURS

The Nazi Party spread octopus-like tentacles through every aspect of German society. However, surprisingly few of the millions of Party members actually wore the NSDAP uniform.

Above: An unusually cheerful Adolf Hitler introduces Benito Mussolini to a Reichsleiter. The golden brown uniforms and gold-braided armbands gave rise to the 'Golden Pheasant' nickname by which senior NSDAP officials were known.

ALL MEMBERS of the National Socialist German Workers Party wore Nazi insignia of one kind or another: all carried Party membership books. But few of those millions of people actually wore the Nazi Party uniform: most were members of subordinate organisations, from the SS and the SA to the RAD and the Hitler Youth.

The wearing of specifically NSDAP uniforms was limited to members of *Das Korps der Politischen Leiter der* NSDAP – The Leadership Corps of the NSDAP. This was the organisation of Nazi party officials, who were divided into seven categories.

THE FÜHRER STATE

The **Führer** was the supreme leader who stood at the top of the party hierarchy. The **Reichsleiter** made up the Party Directorate (*Reichsleitung*). A number of these men, each of whom at some time controlled at least one office in the Party Directorate, were also the heads of party formations and of affiliated or supervised organisations of the party, or of agencies of the state, or held ministerial positions.

Beneath them came the *Hoheitsträger* – the 'bearers of sovereignty'. The 40 or so **Gauleiters** each controlled a *Gau*, an area the size of a county. **Kreisleiters** were the political leaders of the largest subdivision of a Gau. **Ortsgruppenleiter** were responsible for several villages, a town or for part of a larger city, including from 1500 to 3000 households. **Zellenleiter** were the political leaders of a group of from 4 to 8 city blocks or of a corresponding grouping of households in the country. **Blockleiter**, the political leaders of from 40 to 60 households. Each of these *Hoheitsträger* was directly responsible to the next highest leader in the Nazi hierarchy. The Gauleiters were directly subordinate to the Führer himself.

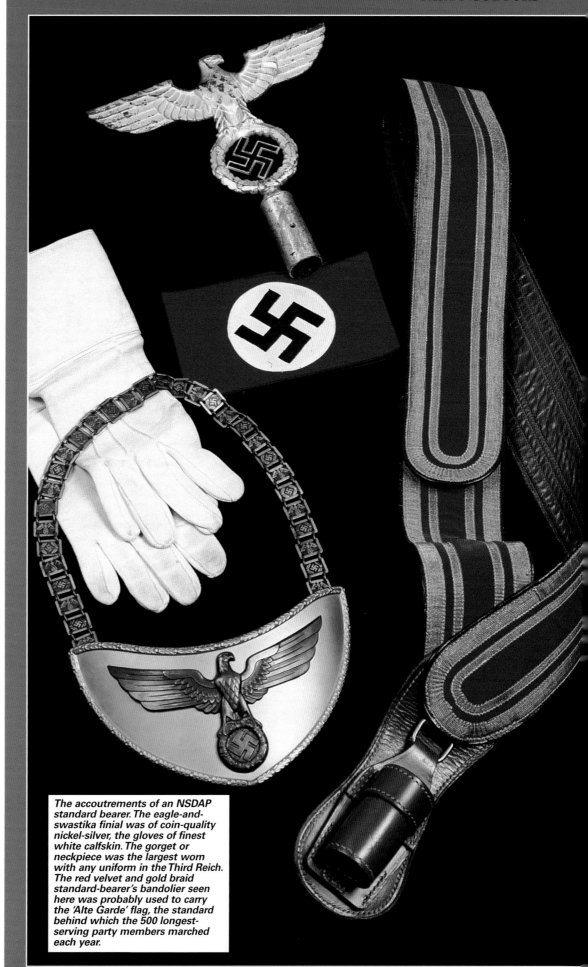

The accoutrements of an NSDAP standard bearer. The eagle-and-swastika finial was of coin-quality nickel-silver, the gloves of finest white calfskin. The gorget or neckpiece was the largest worn with any uniform in the Third Reich. The red velvet and gold braid standard-bearer's bandolier seen here was probably used to carry the 'Alte Garde' flag, the standard behind which the 500 longest-serving party members marched each year.

GOLDEN PHEASANTS OF THE NSDAP

While the Reichsleiter were concerned mainly with policy, the *Hoheitsträger*, from the Gauleiter down, were the face of the Party that ordinary citizens would see most often. The Gauleiter was the political leader of the largest subdivision of the State. He was charged by the Führer with political, cultural, and economic control over the life of the people, which he was to coordinate with the National Socialist ideology

The Führer himself appointed all Gauleiter and Kreisleiter, all Reichsleiter, and all other political leaders within the Reichsleitung (Party Directorate) down to the grade of Gauamtsleiter, the head of a subdivision of the party organisation within a Gau.

The Hoheitsträger and Reichsleitung together constituted the powerful group of leaders by means of which the Nazi party reached into the lives of the people, consolidated its control over them, and compelled them to conform to the National Socialist pattern. For this purpose, broad powers were given them, including the right to call upon all party machinery to effectuate their plans. They could requisition the services of the SA and of the SS, as well as of the HJ and the NSKK.

Below: A group of party insignia. Anti-clockwise from top left they include: party photographer armband (metal plaque has photographer's official permit number); gold cap insignia (post 1938); NSDAP press, head editor's armband; cuffband worn by assistant to Reichsleiter; kreisgericht cuffband worn by legal official working in a town court; a Gauleiter's collar patches; a parade belt made from golden woven celluloid on a brown velvet backing; and a Reichsleiter's armband originally issued to Martin Bormann.

A Gauleiter's peaked cap, identifiable by the red piping and golden embroidered oakleaves; a Gauleiter's car pendant; and a hand-embroidered funeral sash.

Above left: A double-breasted walking-out tunic originally made for Kreis Hauptgemeinschaftsleiter de König who was based in what is now the Czech Republic.

Left: Tunic tailored in Italy for political leader Oswald Zöschg. Based at Merano, Italy Zöschg was a member of Ausland Organisation Ortsgruppe Italian, which acted as a liaison between the NSDAP and Mussolini's Blackshirts.

Right: Clockwise from top left – a Political Leader's NSDAP membership book; a citation for the Gold Party Badge; a cased pair of Gold Party Badges (large for uniform tunic, small for civilian lapel); cover of NSDAP membership book; 25/15/10-year long-service medals; cased Blood Order 2nd series (given to those who took part in the 1934 Austrian putsch. Centre, left to right: Sudetenland badge; NSDAP provisional membership card; Coburg badge for those who fought in an early party battle with the socialists.

LUFTWAFFE

In the six years from 1933, the Luftwaffe grew from absolutely nothing to become one of the largest, best-equipped and most powerful air arms in the world.

THE EARLY LUFTWAFFE was formed almost as soon as the Nazis came to power, though it was kept a clandestine organisation for about two years. It was brought out into the open in 1935 when Hitler overthrew the limits imposed on German military expansion by the Teaty of Versailles. By this time it already had more than 1,000 aircraft and a strength of more than 20,000 personnel.

Expansion was rapid, with modern aircraft being deployed in great numbers. Many were tested for the first time in the Spanish Civil War, when the German *Legion Kondor* supported Franco. The Spanish combat lessons stood Germany in good stead by the time a general European war opened in 1939, and the Luftwaffe proved itself to bc a highly effectve unit, especially in its primary role, which was the support of advancing troops on the ground.

By the beginning of the conflict, there were around 1,500,000 men in Luftwaffe Uniform. Only 50,000 were aircrew: there were another 100,000 in signals, 160,000 in headquarters, administrative, maintenance and construction jobs about 200,000 in training, and a massive 900,000 manning the anti-aircraft guns of the Reich's air defences.

Right: Fighter ace Adolph Galland waits in readiness during the Battle of Britain. Over his lightweight uniform tunic he is wearing the lined leather flying suit essential for high altitude operations, and the ensemble is topped by the typically jaunty Luftwaffe cap.

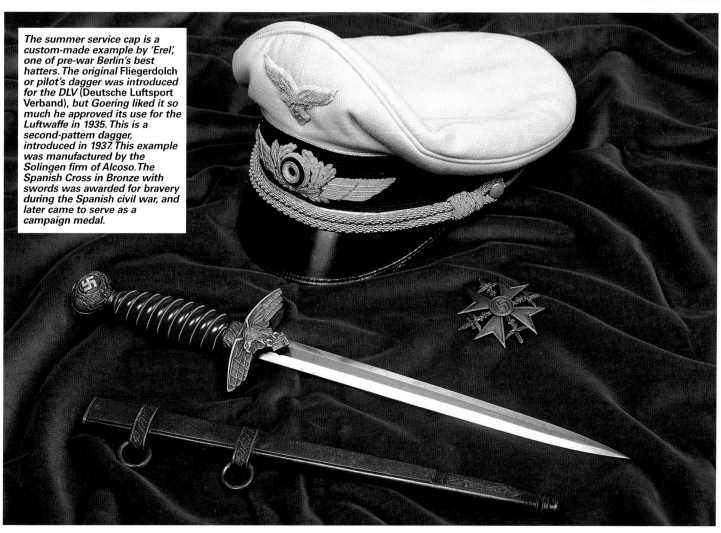

The summer service cap is a custom-made example by 'Erel', one of pre-war Berlin's best hatters. The original Fliegerdolch or pilot's dagger was introduced for the DLV (Deutsche Luftsport Verband), but Goering liked it so much he approved its use for the Luftwaffe in 1935. This is a second-pattern dagger, introduced in 1937. This example was manufactured by the Solingen firm of Alcoso. The Spanish Cross in Bronze with swords was awarded for bravery during the Spanish civil war, and later came to serve as a campaign medal.

Left: The Luftwaffe Corps of Engineers provided the flight engineers for Luftwaffe bombers and transports. The rank collar patches include those for (clockwise from left) an Oberingenieur, Hauptingenier, and Stabsingenieur (Senior Lieutenant, Captain and Major/Colonel)

Right: A pilot's badge, wrist compass, pilot's wristwatch and logbook rest on a 1940-era map of northeast France and the English Channel.

Left: The Luftwaffe controlled a significant number of ground troops, including nearly a million Flak personnel. The Hermann Goering combat division was formed in North Africa in 1942, where it was almost totally destroyed. Reformed as a Panzer division in 1943, it was heavily involved in the Italian campaign.

CAVALRY OF THE CLOUDS

The *Deutsche Luftsports Verband* (German Air Sport Association) was the body by which Germany, forbidden an air force under the Treaty of Versailles, allowed its young citizens to gain experience with flying. DLV members wore a blue uniform, with distinctive rank badges. When the Luftwaffe came into the open in 1935, most of its cadre personnel had come from the DLV, and it made sense to adapt the DLV uniform and insignia for the new air force.

The uniform was similar to that of Britain's Royal Air Force, though few RAF officers wore the riding boots and breeches which were part of the Luftwaffe officer's kit!

Things were much less formal on operations, with other ranks wearing a simple cotton drill uniform or black coveralls. Aircrew wore a lightweight version of their tunic or the comfortable Fliegerbluse, a short jacket with concealed buttons designed to be worn under the flying suit. Paratroop combat uniform included a loose camouflage smock and jump boots.

Below: A four-pocket officers tunic carries a Hauptmann's (Captain's) insignia with a pilot's badge on the left breast pocket. The owner was a veteran – the ribbon bar over the pocket carries a number of World War I awards, including the Iron Cross First Class.

Below: The uniform tunic with white lapels was only worn by General officers in informal full-dress, undress and walking-out uniform. This tunic originally belonged to Generalmajor Schütze, who was stationed in Prague for most of the war.

Above: Three postcards of Luftwaffe Knights Cross holders, produced by Heinrich Hoffmann, together with three colour cards of Luftwaffe subjects by the artist Willrich. Luftwaffe pilots were popular heroes in Germany, and these cards were avidly collected by the children of the period.

Above: The Luftwaffe dress sword was of a late-medieval/early renaissance pattern. Many were made in the traditional steel town of Solingen, but this example was manufactured by Gebrüder Heller in the town of Marienthal.

Left: Luftwaffe Fallschirmjäger or paratroopers were the first airborne forces to see action, dropping in Norway, Belgium and Holland. However, losses in the great parachute assault on Crete were so high that even though the island was captured, paratroopers were never again used in their designed role. Instead, they were used as elite ground troops. This group has an early helmet (later versions lacked the Luftwaffe Eagle and Swastika decal), a 'gravity knife' switchblade, a jump qualification badge and an ammunition bandolier.

Left: One of the most characteristic items in the Luftwaffe officer's uniform inventory was the peaked cap, invariably with the rim folded down fighter-pilot style. The gold piping and braid identifies this as a General's cap, which is shown along with brocade parade belt, a breast eagle and a Generaloberst's collar tabs. Lower-ranking officers wore a similar cap without the gold braid.

Right: The standard Luftwaffe NCO's cap was similar but with less expensive adornments. The yellow piping around the cap indicates that the wearer was flight crew. The Soldbuch beneath was the German soldier's identity card and service record. This example belonged to an NCO stationed in Paris.

THE FÜHRER'S BODYGUARD

Easily the most visible of all of the many branches of the Nazi party, the SS grew from being a small, black clad elite guard in the 1930s to an army of immense fighting power at the end of the War.

Above: Members of SS Panzer Division Das Reich *rest after the battle to retake Kharkhov in March 1943. By this time, most of their equipment is similar to that worn by the Wehrmacht, though they retain their Waffen SS insignia and headgear.*

Left: Standard bearers of the Leibstandarte *on parade. They are wearing the field grey uniform issued to armed SS units in 1938.*

THE HISTORY of the SS falls into distinct phases. Formed as a security force to keep order at party meetings, then becoming the Führer's bodyguard, the SS was not a large organization in the 1920s. By the time Hitler came to power, however, it had grown to around 25,000 men, though this was drop in the ocean compared to the millions of SA members.

BLACKSHIRTS

After 1933, the SS grew rapidly, in the process splitting into three main groups. The *Allgemeine SS* or 'general' SS initially took control of the police and security forces. It was also responsible for administering the rapidly-growing SS economic empire, and took a leading role in investigating and promoting Himmler's racial theories. The *Allgemeine* SS retained the characteristic black unifom long after other SS branches had switched to grey.

Separate from the *Allgemeine* SS, the *Totenkpfverbande* were the camp guards, and have been most responsible for horrible reputation the SS has kept since the end of the war.

SS SOLDIERS

The *Waffen SS* or armed SS was established to provide well-trained troops of unquestioned loyalty to the Party and the Führer. Originally looked on with distrust by the army, as it grew it was absorbed into the regular armed services. In the early days at least its members retained the fanaticism which had been bred into them, which they translated into fighting spirit. However, all-too often that fanaticism translated into war crimes, since fanatics are more prone to brutality than ordinary soldiers.

But as the war went on, it became harder to distinguish the SS from the soldiers alongside whom they served.

Above: Hitler's bodyguard, the Leibstandarte, was first authorised to wear a white summer uniform in June 1939. It was meant to be used between the beginning of April and the end of September, but other than on ceremonial duty at Berchtesgaden it was seldom seen. The tie clip was for civilian wear.

Left: A pair of shoulder straps worn by a Waffen-SS infantry Hauptsturmführer (equivalent to a captain in the British or US armies). The 'Das Reich' cuff title was worn by the second SS division, formed from the SS-VT (Verfügugstruppe) which had fought in France. Renamed 'Reich' in the Balkans, it became 'Das Reich' in Russia in May 1942.

THE BLACK CORPS

From the first, the SS had differentiated itself from the SA by wearing black caps and adopting its own insignia. However, when Himmler was appointed its commander on 6 January 1929, those changes became more profound. Above all, it was the adoption of the all-black uniform with silver trim which made the SS stand out even more from the brown-shirted masses of the SA. To this ready visibility was added fiercely high selection standards and strict training emphasising loyalty to the Führer. It was with this body of men that Hitler seized police power when the Reichstag was burned down, and it was the SS which decapitated the rival SA in the infamous 'Night of the Long Knives'.

Above: Most sections of the NSDAP had their own newspaper. Some, like the SA's Der SA-Mann, had huge circulations. The SS newspaper was Das Schwarze Korps, edited by Guenther D'Alquen. While much of its content highlighted the purity of blood required in the SS world view, it also ran a series of articles in the 1930s calling for Jews to be resettled in Israel.

Below left: Scharführer's tunic of the Leibstandarte, Hitler's SS bodyguard. On the breast is an SA gold sports badge. In the 1930s only the fittest served in the SS and the best went into the Leibstandarte.

Below: Black greatcoat worn by a Scharführer (sergeant) serving with the 3rd Standarte of regiment of the armed SS, Der Führer. This was one of three regiments which, during World War II, would form the core of the SS division Das Reich.

Above: The SS were among the first military units to adopt camouflage uniforms. Badges of rank were redesigned and toned down to match. These arm badges were worn by an Oberführer in the Leibstandarte, equivalent to a senior colonel or brigadier in other armies.

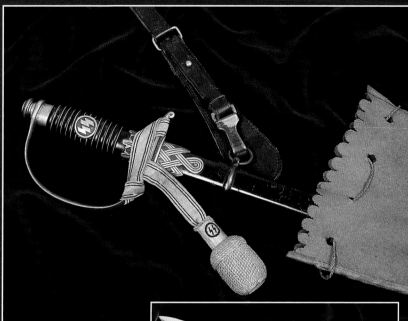

Above: A standard pattern of SS swords was introduced in 1936. Officers did not automatically receive the right to wear one. Himmler would only permit them to be worn by senior members of the Allgemeine SS and graduates of the SS leadership schools.

Right: An early 1933 pattern SS dagger, bearing the SS motto Meine Ehre Heißt Treue (My honour is loyalty). From 1936 the sheaths for such daggers were hung from the belt by an ornate chain.

Above: The Soldbuch or paybook was meant to be carried at all times. It was the SS man's identity card, his service record, and gave details of his current pay, posting and unit.

Right: SS Death's Head rings were awarded to senior officers as a sign of their good standing within the SS. On death, the ring bearer's family could keep the personal citation from Himmler but had to return the ring to the SS.

MEDALS AND ORDERS

Orders, medals and honour insignia were extremely important symbols in the Third Reich, Easily recognisable, the decorations on a uniform provided an instant history of the wearer.

Right: General Fritz Bayerlein as an Afrika Korps Oberstleutnant. He wears a Knight's Cross, an Iron Cross First Class, a wound badge and a tank assault badge.

MEDALS, AWARDS and decorations have always played a significant part in military pageantry. Special badges and insignia are awarded for bravery and achievement, for long service and technical skills, for campaigns and as regimental honours. But in Hitler's Germany they acquired an importance rarely seen in history.

Insignia and awards in the Third Reich were not the preserve of the military alone. The Nazi Party spread its tentacles through every branch of German society, and while its uniforms may have lacked the peacock colours and almost 'ruritanian' style of contemporary Italian designs, the variety of badges, awards, honour weapons and insignia used by the Party was almost infinite.

Right: Stuka pilot Hans Ulrich Rudel was the most highly decorated German soldier of the war. In 2530 combat missions he destroyed more than 500 Soviet tanks. He was awarded the Knight's Cross with Golden Oakleaves (the only recipient), Swords and Diamonds. His gunner wears the German Cross in Gold.

In addition to military awards from World War I there were medals, orders, medallions and badges to commemorate special occasions such as the Nuremberg Rallies and the Olympic Games of 1936.

Everyone in any kind of official position wore a distinctive uniform, from the armed forces and the SS through the Party, the Hitler Youth and the SA to the Postal Service, the Fire Service, the Railway Police and the German Red Cross.

With those uniforms they wore equally distinctive rank and unit insignia and decorations, which immediately identified their position in society and within their own organisation. Party symbols were very important, especially those worn by the *Alte Kameraden* who had been part of the struggle since the early days.

MILITARY MEDALS

As with other armed forces, awards were given for courage in the face of the enemy. The most important was the *Eisernes Kreuz* or Iron Cross, awarded in two classes. It is estimated that around five million Second-Class and half a million First Class crosses were awarded during World War II.

For conspicuous gallantry or outstanding leadership in battle, the Führer also instituted a new class of the cross. Only 7,300 examples of the *Ritterkreuz* or Knight's Cross of the Iron Cross were awarded, and holders became instant heroes. The Knight's Cross made provision for repeat awards, with additional grades being denoted by Oakleaves; Oakleaves and Swords; Oakleaves, Swords and Diamonds; and (uniquely to Hans Ulrich Rudel) Golden Oakleaves, Swords and Diamonds.

The other military awards most commonly worn were the war and combat badges, awarded to troops who had completed a certain number of assaults or who had been on active service for a specified period of time.

Above: The German Cross was instituted on 28 September 1941. It was awarded for distinction in military leadership, though not in the face of the enemy. Ranking between the Iron Cross and the Knight's Cross, it was awarded in two classes: the German Cross in Gold (seen here, 'Gold' referring to the colour of the wreath) for those already holding the Iron Cross, and the German Cross in Silver for holders of the War Merit Cross First Class.

Left: The Iron Cross was instituted in Prussia in 1813. Awarded for gallantry in the face of the enemy, it has been re-introduced for every Prussian and German War since. Adolf Hitler, a holder of the Iron Cross First Class from World War I, revived the award on 1 September 1939. This is an Iron Cross First Class, complete with case and packaging.

COMBAT AWARDS

Left: Luftwaffe Fallschirmjäger badge, issued to qualified parachutists.

Below: Luftwaffe pilot's badge, first awarded on 26 March 1936. Awarded to those successfully completing training as combat pilots.

IN THE FACE OF THE FOE

Combat badges were important symbols of a fighting man's proficiency at his trade, and when worn they gave a complete picture of the wearer's combat experience.

Most took a similar form: An oak wreath surmounted by an eagle with a swastika in its claws, with a symbol descriptive of the award inside the wreath. The Eagle varied according to the service, since the Army, the Kriegsmarine and the Luftwaffe each had their own versions of the symbol.

Waffen-SS members generally received army decorations, since they were in essence part of the armed forces. The only exception was the anti-partisan badge designed by Himmler and first awarded in January 1944. This had no eagle and incorporated a sun-wheel (circular) swastika, a dagger and a Totenkopf, or death's head.

In general, the badges were of very high quality, though towards the end of the war much cheaper material began to be used in their manufacture.

Above left: Silver Tank Destruction Strip, awarded for the single-handed destruction of an enemy tank. A gold award was also issued, for the solo destruction of five or more tanks.

Above: Silver Close-Combat Clasp, awarded for participation in 30 days of hand-to-hand fighting without armoured support. A Gold clasp was awarded for 50 days of close-quarters combat, with a Bronze award for 15 days of infantry action.

Below: The High Seas Fleet badge was instituted by the Kriegsmarine on 30 April 1941. It was awarded to the crews of battleships and cruisers who completed 12 weeks of active service at sea.

Far left: Luftwaffe Flak Badge. It was awarded to flak crews who achieved 16 qualifying points, four points being awarded for each enemy aircraft brought down by an individual battery and two for aircraft shared by several batteries.

Left: The Infantry Assault badge was awarded to soldiers who had taken part in at least three infantry actions on three separate days.

Below: Originally dating from 1918, the Wound Badge was reinstituted in May 1939. It came in Gold for five or more wounds suffered in combat, Silver (as seen here) for three or four, and Black for one or two.

NAZI PORCELA

The SS had its fingers in many pies, but one of the most unusual was the porcelain factory it owned at Allach, near Dachau.

The figure of Athena, modelled by Professor T.H. Karner, was produced by the Allach factory to commemorate the 'Day of German Art' in Munich in 1938. The box carried a variant of the the city's coat of arms, together with the legend 'Munich, Capital of the Movement'.

GERMAN ARTISTS and craftsmen have always been amongst the finest producers of European porcelain. During the Third Reich, such names as Meissen and Nymphenburg were joined by another producer – SS-Porcelain Allach, located on the outskirts of Munich.

The Allach factory was started in 1933 at the instigation of Reichsführer SS Heinrich Himmler. Originally privately owned, the Allach Factory was one of the first industrial enterprises taken over by the SS when the 'Black Corps' began building up its economic interests Unlike other SS businesses, however, it was not transferred to the WVHA, the main economic office of the SS, but remained under the control of Himmler's own office, the *Personlicher Stab, Reichsführer SS.*

With the financial backing of the SS, the Allach factory could attract some of the top craftsmen of the time away from established firms like Rosenthal and Meissen.

DACHAU WORKERS

Later, during the war, the factory was able to make use of its proximity to Dachau concentration camp as a source of cheap labour for heavy manual work. However, the factory was not a slave-labour enterprise like the SS sword maker which was established within Dachau itself.

Allach's output included a large number of Nazi items, but it was far from being the only porcelain factory producing such goods. Commemorative plates, plaques, cups, goblets and statuettes were sold in huge numbers to the general public by all of the major manufacturers.

Above: SS-Porcelain Allach produced a large number of animal figures, dogs being a particular speciality. But dogs were not the only figures produced: this bear is modelled on the animal featured on the coat of arms of the city of Berlin. Such wares were sold to the general public through retailers of fine porcelain

Above: Himmler's personal interests in German and Germanic history encouraged most of the major porcelain factories to produce figures inspired by folklore. This example, produced by the leading firm of Rosenthal in the 1930s, represents a traditional historic figure known as the Bamberg Reiter or the 'Bamberg Rider'. Historic figures were very much in vogue during the early years of the Third Reich, and they sold very well.

Designed by sculptor Ottmar Obermeier, the Allach figure of 'The Fencer' was one of the few pieces the factory sold with a 'biscuit' or unglazed finish. In 1941, Prague artist painted a portrait of Reinhard Heydrich with an example of the Allach Fencer in the background, as a reference to the SD leader's interest in the sport.

Above: A candlestick designed by Carl Diebitsch for the SS factory is typical of the domestic products produced at Allach. It incorporates a runic sun motif.

Below: Allach bowl produced for the Reichsführer's guests at the 1937 Reichsparteitag. Apples were much favoured for such bowls: the SS recreation of pagan rituals placed great emphasis on sun worship, and red apples were seen as symbols of the sun.

Above: A flower vase manufactured by the old-established Bavarian firm of Nymphenburg. It was made to commemorate the towns of Pasing, Grosshadern and Feldmoching becoming part of Munich.

Below: An Allach porcelain plate produced as a commemorative item for the Julfest (the pagan Yule festival, celebrated by the SS in place of Christmas.) Manufactured late in 1943, the plate is of very high quality, with the moulded eagle in the centre being particularly fine.

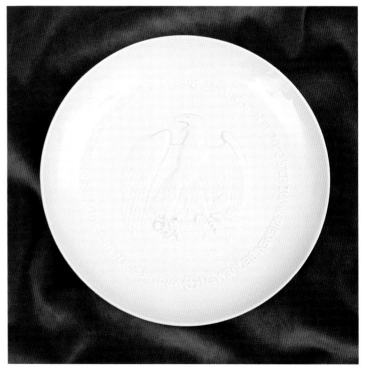

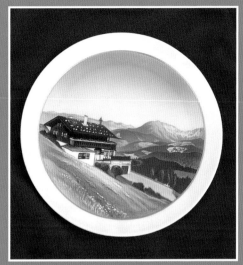

PARTY MEMORIES

From the very beginning of its manufacture in Europe, high-quality china has been used for decoration as much as – if not more than – for eating and drinking. From the 19th century, commemorative porcelain pieces have been manufactured to celebrate great events. With the rise of tourism in the 20th century, a new market opened up with the production of souvenirs and mementos of famous places.

The Third Reich saw the production of large numbers of such souvenirs. Many were bought by ordinary citizens purely for ornament. However, there was also a thriving trade in souvenirs at the great party rallies at Nuremberg. In addition, there were specifically party pieces, deliberately archaic in form, which were designed to link the organisations of the Third Reich with ancient Germanic traditions.

Above left: A limited edition Meissen plate produced for members of the Luftwaffe involved in the drive on Moscow in 1941. The plates were hand-painted before firing.

Above centre: A limited edition, hand-painted Rosenthal plate showing Hitler's Berghof retreat on the Obersalzberg at Berchtesgaden. These plates were made from 1933, and this example shows the house as it was before it was extended in the later 1930s.

Above right: A commemorative plate by the old-established firm of Villeroy & Boch. It has a print of the Brown House, the Munich headquarters of the NSDAP, together with a shield bearing the coat of arms of the city of Munich.

Right: An earthenware Julleuchter, or Yule candlestick. Based on archaic pot designs, the Julleuchter were given as gifts to selected SS men by Reichsführer Heinrich Himmler on the occasion of the Winter Solstice, a major festival in the neo-pagan rituals introduced by the SS.

Below left: A Luftwaffe honour goblet, awarded by Reichsmarschall Hermann Goering to Stuka pilot Leutnant Hernert Eichblatt . Such goblets were given to aircrew who showed extreme bravery in the air.

Below right: An mass-produced propaganda piece from the early 1930s, showing a Bavarian SA man and the Party slogan "Deutschland Erwache".

PARTY FAVOURS

Almost every organisation in the Third Reich – even the civilian ones – had their own uniforms. And wherever uniforms are worn, you will also see a lot of medals, orders and decorations.

Unlike most Nazi leaders, Heinrich Himmler had no World War I experience. He was acutely aware of his lack of combat decorations, and tried to compensate by wearing party awards. Here, the Reichsführer sports two of the most important Nazi decorations – the Party Badge in Gold at the centre of his left breast pocket and the ribbon of the Blood Order – only worn by those who took part in the 1923 Beerhall Putsch – in his right buttonhole. The medal beneath the party badge is a bronze sports qualification badge.

NATIONAL Socialists had awards for just about everything. There were medals for long service and good conduct, and medals for bearing children. Awards were given for long party membership, and for exceptional service. There were sports medals and proficiency awards, mementoes of Party rallies and of notable street battles with the Socialists.

Medals serve a number of distinct functions. Whatever your line of work in Hitler's Germany, there was probably a medal for exemplary performance of your duties. But they were more than rewards for service.

Groups who see themselves as 'different' have always used regalia to enhance their identity – from civic dignitaries and masonic lodges to churches and the military.

Each piece of adornment on Nazi uniforms had a message. The combination of uniform, medals, badges and symbols of rank gave an instant picture of just who you were and where you stood in the Nazi hierarchy. It was not unique to Germany, but what was unique to the Third Reich was the extent to which the Party and its awards penetrated every level of Hitler's Reich.

Above: The Eagle Order (properly, the Meritorious Order of the German Eagle) was instituted on 1 May 1937. It was the highest German award for foreigners, and was designed to be conferred upon visiting statesmen and prominent personalities in friendly countries. Six classes of award existed: The Third Class Award (seen here with and without swords) was worn at the neck, while the Fifth Class Award (seen here with swords) was worn on a breast ribbon.

Right: Very different from the rare awards to prominent foreigners, but far more common were the assorted gifts, souvenirs and memorabilia of party occasions. Seen here are an NSDAP notebook and souvenir pen dating from the early 1930s, a party badge imitating an SA Feldzeichen or Standard, a Party membership badge, a badge worn at the Westfalen party meeting in 1936, and a gold medallion commemorating the tenth anniversary of the first Party Day in Weimar.

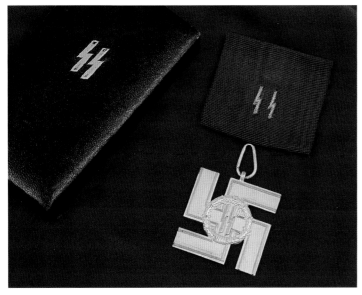

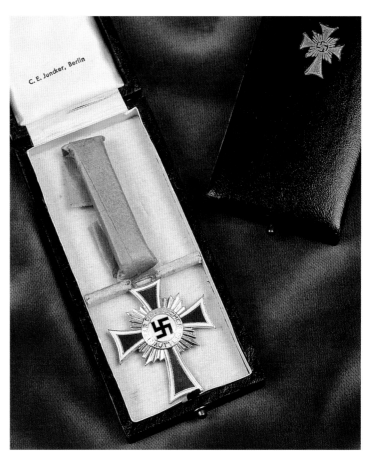

Above: The SS long service award was instituted on 30 January 1938. Four- and eight-year awards were medals: the 12-year award shown here was a hakenkreuz *in silver. If the Third Reich had lasted long enough, the 25-year award would have been the same in Gold.*

Right: The Nazis venerated motherhood, and had a special award for especially fertile women. The Cross of Honour of the German Mother was awarded in Bronze for four or five children, silver for six or seven and gold (as seen here) for bearing eight children or more.

Below: The Faithful Service Cross was instituted under the Weimar Republic, but was honoured under the Third Reich. It was awarded to members of the Public Services who had worked for the same concern continuously for 25, 40 or 50 years.

PARTY COMMEMORATIONS

Mass meetings were fundamental to the character of National Socialist Germany. Although the *Parteitage* started in a small way in the 1920s, by the time Hitler came to power in 1933 they had become massive spectaculars. Smaller versions also took place in every region, city and town in Germany.

In a state where following the party line was essential for success, it became politic to wear some sort of emblem to show that you had done your bit for the party. There were plenty to choose from: every meeting of this kind had a badge to wear, usually fairly cheaply stamped out by the thousand and made from cheap plastic, tin plate or aluminium.

Above left: The Party awarded medals to anybody who took part in the Blumenkriege – the bloodless occupations of territory in 1938 and 1939. The silver Medaille zur Erinnerung an den 13 März 1938 commemorates the Anschluss with Austria, while the bronze Medaille zur Erinnerung an den 1 October 1938 was given to those who occupied the Sudetenland.

Above right: The Goldenes Parteiabzeichen or Gold Party Badge could only be worn by the first 100,000 members of the Nazi Party. The largest version was worn on the left breast pocket in uniform; the smaller badge was worn as a lapel button in civilian clothing. The standard party member's badge was smaller without the wreath. It was generally worn as a tie pin in uniform dress.

Right: Party rallies were amongst the most important occasions in the National Socialist calendar. In addition to the massive national party days at Nuremberg, each Gau or administrative district held its own Gautage, usually but not always in June. These badges (clockwise starting top left) are from Süd-Hanover Braunschweig in 1936, Koblenz-Trier in 1935, Schleswig-Holstein in 1936, Karlsruhe in 1937 and Süd-Hanover Braunschweig in 1938.

Below: Each Gau consisted of several Kreise or districts. These usually held a Kreistage a couple of weeks before the Gautage. Being smaller affairs, their badges were often cheaply produced out of plastic. These badges commemorate meetings at Cologne in 1939, Ammerland in 1939, Mindelheim in 1935, Iserlohn in 1936 and (centre) Cologne in 1935.

THE NAZI EAGLE

THE GERMAN eagle, grim in stone or bronze, vied with the swastika as the most potent symbol of the Third Reich. On uniforms, equipment, weapons, documents, coinage – in fact on almost every artefact produced during the years of the Third Reich either the swastika or the eagle (frequently both) was stamped, printed, painted or engraved.

ARYAN SYMBOL

Hitler and the Nazis regarded the eagle as an Aryan symbol, and combined with the swastika it formed the national emblem. The most common designs were either an eagle with wings spread, often known as the Wehrmachtadler or with wings partly folded, which was known as the Reichsadler.

HISTORIC ORIGINS

The origins of the eagle as a German national emblem can be traced back to 800 AD when Charlemagne was crowned Roman emperor and adopted the eagle, which had been the totem of the all-conquering Roman legions, as his own. From the 12th century the eagle spread through Germany as a symbol of Hohenstaufen dynasty which ruled the Holy Roman Empire, and it regularly appeared on coats of arms of ducal and princely families. It also, in a different form, became the symbol of the Austrian empire.

GERMAN EAGLES

By the 19th century the spread-winged eagle had come to symbolise Germany, and the revolutionaries of 1848, Bismarck's Second Reich of 1871 and the Weimar Republic of 1919 all adopted the symbol as their own.

Left: Even though it was seen on a variety of military uniforms, badges and flags, the eagle with the outstretched wing was primarily a party symbol. This example adorns the cover of an Arbeitsbuch. Introduced in 1934, this was a civilian version of a soldier's soldbuch, and was compulsory for all workers. It contained details of a worker's employment history and work record.

Above: The hilt of an SA dagger is adorned with one of the earliest forms of the Nazi eagle. Much less medieval in appearance than Imperial eagles, it differed primarily from Weimar or earlier versions by its outspread wings.

Above: A wartime Gestapo pass is adorned with an Eagle and Swastika stamp of approval. Even though by this time the Gestapo was a part of the SS security service, the SD, it used the party Eagle rather than the variant generally used by the SS.

Below: Der Deutsches Automobilclub was the premier motoring organisation in the car-mad Germany of the 1920s. It used a variant of the Prussian or Reichsadler, to which was added a swastika when the Nazis came to power.

Below: The upright oval shape of military combat awards lent itself to the use of the folded-wing Weimar-style eagle, which some authorities have called the 'National Eagle' to distinguish it from the 'Party Eagle'.

Below: Although most Nazi Eagles conformed to one of about three or four standard styles, there were some one-off designs. This eagle with spread, pointed wings was used to tip the flag pennant on a senior official's car.

Above: Pre-war Germany was a nation in love with uniforms and symbols. Most large organisations had their own unique style: this is the cap and belt buckle of the German Red Cross. It utilises a variant of the old Weimar eagle, often known as the Reichsadler.

Below: There were many types of German police units, including traffic, railway and water police. This cap was worn by members of the Fire service – which was considered to be a police formation. Most police units wore the style of Eagle seen here.

Above: The Deutscher Luftsportverband was used to train pilots for the clandestine Luftwaffe. When rearmament was announced in 1935, the DLV was replaced by the National Socialist Flying Corps, which wore a Luftwaffe-style uniform but with a variant of the Party eagle.

Below: Some Nazi eagles were more impressive than others. This large silver-thread cap variant was worn (outside the court room) by senior members of the Supreme Court. Nominally independent, the Justice Ministry worked hand-in-hand with the party and with the SS.

Left: The Luftwaffe's symbol differed from the Army's adler: it was a more natural eagle in flight. Unique to the air force, it was used on helmets in place of the Reichsadler, and was used as breast and arm badges in place of the Heeresadler and Party Eagle. This is a Luftwaffe helmet, as used by Flak batteries and by Luftwaffe ground combat troops in Italy and on the Eastern Front.

Right: The insignia of a senior sergeant or oberfeldwebel. The yellow piping and badge indicate that the wearer was an aircrewman. The 'Boelcke' cuff title was worn in 1935 by Flieger Gruppe Fassberg, one of the early bomber units of the Luftwaffe.

IN NAZI GERMANY the eagle normally grasped in its claws an oak wreath garland which surrounded the swastika. The Heer (Army) and the Kriegsmarine (Navy) wore the Wehrmachtadler on the left breast of their tunics with a smaller version on officers and NCO's caps above the traditional red, white and black cockade.

The Luftwaffe used a slightly different symbol: an eagle with its wings curved in flight clutching a swastika in its talons. It was similar in some respects to the Royal Air Force eagle, though the British bird flew to left, while that of the Luftwaffe flew to the right. The Luftwaffe eagle was worn by air and ground crew and by the paratroopers and anti-aircraft gunners who were part of the air force.

The SS wore their eagle and swastika on the upper left sleeve of their tunics. Though similar to the Wehrmachtadler the shape of the outer edges of the wings was different.

The Army, Kriegsmarine, Luftwaffe, and Waffen-SS all wore leather belts with a metal buckle featuring a variant of the National Emblem. The Army retained the old Imperial motto Gott mit Uns – 'God with Us'– on the buckle. The SS saw Christianity as Jewish by origin, however, and used the motto Meine Ehre Heisst Treue – 'My Honour is Loyalty'.

One of the more unusual manifestations of the National Emblem was on the aluminium gorget worn by the Army Feldgendarmerie or military police. The gorget hung around their necks on a nickel chain and earned military policemen the nickname 'chain dogs'. It was silver coloured with the words Felgendarmerie on a grey scroll. The letters, rivets securing the chain and national emblem were finished with luminous paint, particularly useful on traffic control duties at night.

At the head of the nation stood Adolf Hitler, the man whose drive for power spread the swastika and eagle across most of Europe. Curiously, in a nation which thrived on uniforms, his personal style was modest. He generally wore a simple military-style four pocket tunic or informal blazer-style uniform jacket, unadorned except for the Wehrmachtadler on the sleeve and his Iron Cross and Party Badge on the breast.

MILITARY EAGLES

Left: An Early SS cap dating from about 1932 shows the Prussian-style deathshead typical of the time, together with an eagle similar to those used by police units. Later the SS would have its own unique insignia.

Right: The SS uniform eagle was similar to those used by the Army and navy, though with slightly different wing tips. However the SS stamp used to validate this SS man's Soldbuch carries a standard party-style eagle, with rounded trailing edges to the bird's wings.

Right: The armed forces agreed to wear Nazi symbols in 1934. The most prominent insignia were the eagles worn on caps and as breast badges. The Heeresadler or army eagle was based on the party eagle, but with longer, more regular wings and wingtips.

Left: The large arm badge worn by Army standard bearers bore a representation of the regimental standards together with a Weimar-style 'National Eagle'. The pink colours on this example indicate that the wearer was in a Panzer unit. Such eagles were also commonly found in heraldry, and as wall decorations and statues on important buildings and monuments.

SS-POLIZEI

ERMANY WAS a country with a plethora of uniformed police. Traditionally, each of the Lander had their own forces, and local fire services and specialist security units were also under police control. National Socialism saw the creation of a national police service, under the control of SS chief Heinrich Himmler.

Himmler's official title as of June 1936 was *Reichsführer SS und Chef der Deutschen Polizei*. Under his aegis were the security services (Gestapo and SD) under Reinhard Heydrich, which included the plainclothes *Kriminalpolizei* or Kripo under Artur Nebe, and the uniformed *Ordnungspolizei* or Orpo

Left: Kurt Daluege, the head of the **Ordningspolizei** *or uniformed police, takes the salute at an SS parade. Daluege, an Alte Kampfer and former head of the Berlin SA oversaw the creation of a national police force under SS control.*

commanded by former Berlin SA and SS leader Kurt Daluege.

The *Ordnungspolizei* was composed in the main of former members of the various *Landespolizei* together with ex-SA members. Its components included the *Schutzpolizei*, or urban police; the *Schutzpolizei des Gemeinden*, or community police; the *Gendarmerie* or rural police; the *Wasserschutzpolizei* or water/river police; the *Feuerschutzpolizei* or fire service; and various technical, auxiliary and volunteer police units. In 1939 the *Ordnungspolizei* had a strength of 130,000 officers and men.

Special police units were raised as war broke out. These battalions were intended to perform regular police duties in the occupied territories, as well as providing anti-partisan security to the Wehrmacht's lines of communication. By the time the police rifle battalions were transferred to the SS, in 1943, *Ordnungspolizei* strength had risen to 310,000.

Below: Jews are deported from Wurzburg in 1943. They are guarded by uniformed policemen, who by this time are fully integrated into the SS and who also provide combat troops for the Waffen-SS on the Eastern Front.

Above: The traditional German police shako is of a style which dated back to the 19th Century. Up until the 1930s it was the trademark of the uniformed police, much as the British policeman's helmet remains to this day. But by the time war broke out, most police wore standard military-style peaked caps on duty. The only time the shako appeared was in ceremonials, in which case it was often adorned with a plume.

Left: A police officer's visor cap as worn during the war years, together with a parade belt and bayonet. The police cap badge was a variant of the party eagle and swastika enclosed within an oak wreath. It was used by all police formations, and as a decal was applied to the helmets of police formations serving as military or paramilitary units. The belt had interwoven oakleaves and runes in silver brocade, which was applied to a green velvet backing, and was worn by most police units.

Below left: The standard police bayonet had staghorn grips and polished steel fittings. Although a normal military bayonet in form, the hilt was adorned with a traditional hunting motif, the head of an eagle. As with most German edged weapons, the hilt is adorned with the particular badge of the organisation: in this case a small version of the police cap badge. The scabbard was usually of brown leather.

Below: Der Deutsche Polizeibeamte was an official magazine distributed to police administrative departments. It contained news relating to police activities and professional articles about police work. As with most house magazines in the Third Reich, it had a large section devoted to reports of police sporting activities – an important feature even though members of police units were generally older and much less fit than those in military or SS units.

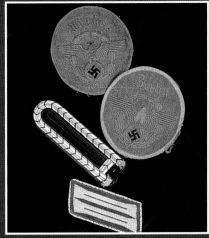

THE SS AND THE POLICE

SS CONTROL OF THE German police did not come in one fell swoop. The original notion of a national police force came from Wilhelm Frick, the Interior minister, and he vied with Himmler for three years for control of Germany's law enforcement bodies. Himmler began by absorbing the Bavarian police, gaining control of the Prussian-based Gestapo after the Night of the Long Knives. In 1936 Himmler became Chief of the German Police, with Reinhard Heydrich in control of the security and plain-clothed organisations and Kurt Daluege in charge of the uniformed branches.

Rivalry between two of Himmler's most powerful subordinates was fierce. The 1939 establishment of the *Reichssicherheitshauptamt* – the RSHA – gave Heydrich greater actual power than Daluege, but the head of the uniformed police maintained the *Hauptamt Ordnungspolizei* as a separate SS department.

Above left: A selection of Schutzpolizei insignia. The wreathed eagle and swastika in silvered metal is from the peaked visor cap. The silver wire-wreathed cloth badge was worn on the upper arm. The epaulette and collar patch indicate that the wearer was a Lieutenant. The small enamel badge, normally worn in the buttonhole of civilian dress, was issued to the Munich police administration in 1937

Above centre: The wreathed eagle and swastika would have been worn on the tunic sleeve. The basic design was common to all Schutzpolizei members, the only change being the name indicating in which city the bearer served. The collar patch and epaulette would have been worn by an Oberwachtmeister or senior non-commissioned officer.

Above right: Although senior police officers were almost invariably members of the SS and had SS ranks, they also carried police ranks. This is the pre-war collar patch worn by police generals in the ranks of Generalmajor, Generalleutnant and General der Polizei. The cap badge and arm badge are the same pattern as those worn by more junior officers, but the cap badge is gilt metal and the arm badge is hand-embroidered gold bullion.

Above: Police Soldbuch or identity book and service record carried by all members of the police service. The medals are a parade set, and include the Iron Cross from World War I. The silver and gold long service medals were awarded for 18 and 25 years in the police.

Right: Rank patches and cuff title for a Brigadeführer und Generalmajor der Waffen SS serving with the SS-Polizei division. Originally formed as a police combat unit in 1939, it came under SS control in 1941 and became the fourth Waffen-SS division in 1942.

NAT·SOZ·DEUTSCHE ARBEITERPARTEI

STURMABTEILUNG

DEUTSCHLAND

ERWACHE

NSKK

LTHOUGH NOT as well-known today as the SA or the SS, the NSKK or *Nationalsozialistisches Kraftfahrkorps* (National Socialist Motor Corps) was one of the Nazi party's senior organisations.

Originally a branch of the SA, it was founded in 1930 as the NSAK (Nazi Automobile Corps). The NSAK's primary function was to provide a vehicle pool – mostly private cars – to assist in the increasing demands of party electioneering. It was renamed the NSKK in 1931, and in 1934 became independent of the SA.

The NSKK's functions changed considerably when the Nazis came to power. One aim was to teach motoring skills to the young, and more than 200,000 teenagers were taught to drive between 1933 and 1939. The NSKK also acted as traffic police, and provided a nationwide breakdown assistance service.

The NSKK – or more precisely, the affiliated *Deutscher Automobil-Club* – was also the only official organiser of motor sports in the Third Reich.

WAR ROLE

As war approached, the NSKK was given a more overtly military mission. It was used to provide transport for the massive engineering projects of the Todt organisation, and had responsibility for instructing army reserve drivers. With the outbreak of war, the NSKK provided logistics support to the Wehrmacht and the Luftwaffe, and units occasionally found themselves in combat.

After its first year the NSKK had a membership of under 10,000: at the time of the invasion of Poland it had grown into a formidable body half a million strong.

Above left: Adolf Hitler uses the **Blutfahne** *to 'consecrate' the* **Feldzeichen** *or banners of the National Socialist Motor Corps. The NSKK, with their distinctive leather helmets, played a part in all major Nazi ceremonials.*

Above: The NSKK's distinctive helmet. Worn primarily as part of the 'Grand Parade' uniform, it was based on the crash helmet originally used by pilots of the Imperial German army's flying service during the First World War. The 'First pattern' helmet worn in the early 1930s bore a stylised nickel-silver eagle. The 'Second pattern' helmet, introduced as membership increased dramatically later in the 1930s, had a cheaper, simpler aluminium eagle and swastika, to which had been added the NSKK scroll. The NSKK dagger was a variant of the standard SA weapon.

Right: Traditionally, Nationalsozialistisches Kraftfahrkorps units were named after the regions in which they were raised. However, after the death of Korpsführer *Adolf Hühnlein* in 1942, Motorgruppe Hochland was given his name as a memorial and wore a dedicated cuff title. The collar patches seen here were those of an NSKK-Gruppenführer *or General.* The silvered eagle is a wartime example, distinguishable from pre-war versions by its longer wingspan.

Right: A pre-war NSKK tan uniform shirt. It was worn by an NSKK Obersturmführer (senior lieutenant) on the staff of of NSKK Motorstandarte (Motor Regiment) 58. This unit was based at Braunschweig and formed part of the Brigade Niedersachsen – which confusingly had the same brown epaulette piping as the Westmark Brigade. The uniform of tan shirt, black 'Sam Brown' belt, black breeches and jackboots was worn on parade before the war: later members of the NSKK on wartime duties wore army-style uniforms.

Below right: A group of items associated with Adolf Hühnlein, the founder and Korpsführer of the NSKK, The group includes a souvenir postcard, his Korpsführer collar tabs, and a signed letter. Hühnlein, a former army engineer and staff officer served in the Freikorps after the war. He joined the SA in 1923 and took part in the Beer Hall Putsch. Hühnlein became party quartermaster in 1925; in 1927 he was made head of the SA motor troops and in 1931 he became the leader of the NSKK. In 1933 Hühnlein was given added responsibility by Hitler, to whom he reported directly. He was to reform the entire German motor industry and to encourage the use of the car by the German people. During the war he organised Germany's motor transport network.

Below: An NSKK four-pocket service tunic. This example was worn by an NSKK Rottenführer (senior corporal) of the 3rd Battalion, NSKK Motorstandarte 151, based at Mannheim. The colour of the piping on the single epaulette indicated the Brigade to which the regiment belonged, brown in this case indicating Brigade Westmark. The NSKK Eagle was worn on the upper right sleeve. The diamond arm insignia on the lower left sleeve is a first pattern qualified driver's insignia.

MOTORISED NAZIS

Above: There was a section of the NS Motor Corps devoted to water transport. Marine NSKK members were identifiable from the gold rather than silver braid used in their insignia. This group shows the sleeve eagle and swastika and the standard sleeve diamond used by motor boat units. The NSKK Marine epaulette is the type worn by junior ranks.

Above left: An NSKK insignia group from the 41st Abteilung, Motorstandarte 81 (usually abbreviated 41/M81 and worn on the right collar tab). The light blue cloth and piping on the triangular forage cap badge and epaulette indicate a unit from Hochland/Bayernwald. The 81st Standarte was based at Regensburg in the Bayernwald.

Below and below left: NSKK forage caps bore both rank insignia and regional identification. The Blue triangle indicated Hansa or Hessen, the brown triangle was worn by brigades in Westmark and Niedersachsen, and the orange triangle was carried by Südwest and Mitte brigades. The rank badges indicate (left to right) NSKK Sturmmann, NSKK Scharführer and NSKK Truppführer. The officer's forage cap with the apple-green triangle from Thüringen or Pommern carries the rank insignia of an Oberstürmführer.

THE ORGANISATION of the NSKK, once it had been separated from the SA, reflected the pyramidal structure typical of Nazi groups. At the head was *Der Führer des NSKK*, or *Korpsführer*, answerable only to Adolf Hitler. The leadership office was responsible for NSKK leadership schools, the technical school in Munich and the technical and equipment inspectorate. Beneath the leadership office were four *Motor-Obergruppen* – Nord, Ost, West and Süd. Each of these, commanded by an *Obergruppen-*führer, controlled a number of *Motor-Gruppen* and *Motor-Brigaden* which in turn were composed of several *Standarte* or regiments. Two independent *Motor-Gruppen*, Ostland and Schlesien, reported direct to the *NSKK Korpsführung*. Each *Motor Standarte* consisted of three or four *Motor-Staffeln* or squadrons, which in turn were made up from up to five *Motor-Stürme*. The organisational structure paralleled that of the SS, and NSKK ranks were similar to those of the black-clad security units.

SS-DOCUMENTS

Heinrich Himmler presents a title deed to the family of peasant farmer Peter Issl. People like these were seen by the Nazis as the life blood of the German volk, and their lands were protected by law.

GERMANY UNDER the Nazis was a land where forms and documentation were a way of life. Extensive records were kept of every citizen, especially in files of the Gestapo.

Everything was recorded, from the monthly donations of party supporters in the 1920s to the records of slain Jews and the plans for the gas chambers and crematoria used in the death camps twenty years later.

The SS was particularly prone to producing an excess of documentation, perhaps reflecting the bureaucratic nature of Himmler. It is in the SS files that one can read the minutes of the Wannsee Conference, which established the 'Final Solution' to the 'Jewish problem.'

But the majority of SS documentation was of a more mundane kind. Every SS member had a number and a membership book: fighting men had a military-style *Soldbuch* (combined paybook and service record).

Right: The 1944 travel pass and identity card of a senior Gestapo official – by this time most secret policemen were in the SS.

Dienstausweis Nr. 221
(Gültig bis 1. 1. 1946)
für
45
Wilhelm Höche,
Kriminalinspektor
beim Geheimen Staatspolizeiamt
Berlin, den 2. Januar 1945
Der Chef der Sicherheitspolizei und des SD
(Unterschrift des Inhabers)

There is a vast range of
collectable SS documentation,
memorabilia and ephemera,
though identifying the genuine
article can sometimes be
difficult. This is a programme for
a pre-war concert given by the
band of the SS-Leibstandarte
Adolf Hitler. The black and silver
'Swallow's Nests' are traditional
shoulder decorations worn by
military bandsmen.

Left: One item no self-respecting SS member could go without was a copy of 'Mein Kampf' – though it is likely that very few actually read it. Originally published in two volumes in 1925 and 1926, it appeared in a single-volume, Bible format edition in 1930. Up to the accession of power in 1933, some 287,000 copies had been sold: after that sales moved into the millions. In December 1939 a Party document suggested that "soon every German family would have a copy of the Führer's work."

Below left: The SS Zivilabzeichen, or civilian lapel badge. Wearing the lapel badge on civilian clothing was not a general right: permission had to be given for each specific individual to wear it. This document gives that right to Christian Weber, an early member of the Nazi Party and a bearer of the 'Blood Order' awarded to those who had taken part in the abortive Munich of November 1923.

Below: Membership book for SS-Förderndes Mitglieder, or 'Supporting Members' of the SS. In order to raise funds for the SS, early leader Joseph Berchtold introduced the concept of SS sponsors in 1926. These were not necessarily full members of the SS, but supported the aims of the organisation by donating a specific sum of money – in this instance, dating from 1934, one Reichsmark per month. As the SS expanded in the early 1930s, many secret supporting members in business and the academic world were persuaded to become full members of the organisation.

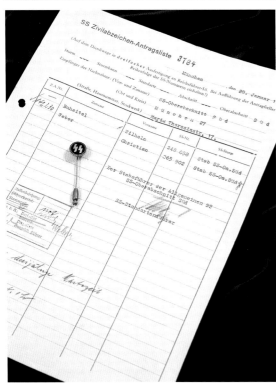

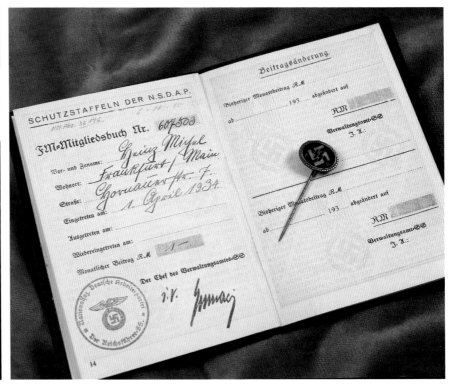

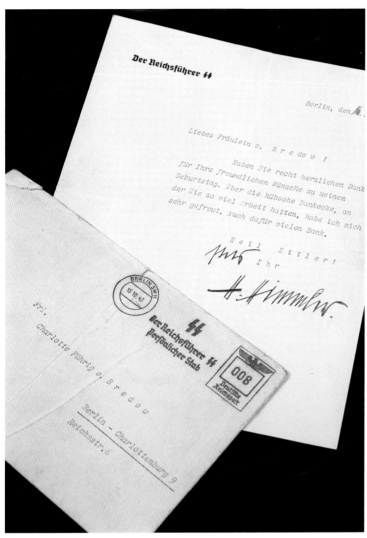

Above: Citation and badge for the Special Honour Lapel Pin of the SS-Heimwehr Danzig. The lapel pin was issued on 10 October 1939, just over a month after the outbreak of war. It was awarded to all members of the SS in the free port of Danzig who took part in the siezure of the city on the first day of the Polish campaign.

Below: An SS-Man's pocket diary for 1944. These small diaries were standard issue to SS troops. They were organised with two days to a page, and had additional colour plates at the back which depicted Army, SS and political insignia. The diary rests on a citation for the Infantry Assault Badge, awarded to SS-Rottenführer (Corporal) Willi Jöckel in August 1942. Soldiers who had taken part in three infantry attacks were eligible for the badge. The bronze version seen here was awarded to motorised troops: infantry and mountain troops wore a silver badge.

Above: A personal letter, dated 16 October 1940, from the Reichsführer-SS Heinrich Himmler to the Countess von Bredow. In the letter he thanks her for the birthday card she sent, and aologises for the briefness of the reply, pleading pressure of work.

Below: Money from Buchenwald. These tokens were used by the SS-Totenkopf guards in the camp but could only be exchanged for goods in the staff canteen. The distinctive Death's Head collar patch and brown epaulette piping were used by all camp guards.

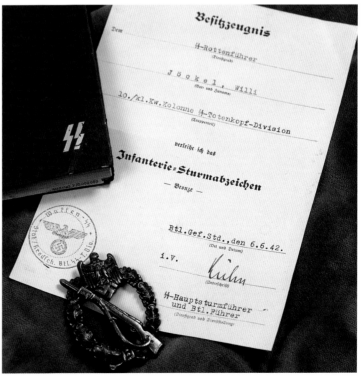

Left and Below: Adolf Hitler consecrates the Feldzeichen or standards of new SA Standarten at Nuremberg. Ritual played an important part in each of the Reichsparteitage, but the gatherings were almost as much about being a huge public holiday. At least as many ordinary Germans gathered to watch the festivities as came to take part.

NUREMBERG hosted the annual congresses of the Nazi Party not only because it was an early National Socialist stronghold, but also because it was the meeting place of Germanic emperors in the medieval period. Unlike the annual meetings of other political parties, which were annual discussions to set political agenda and objectives, the *Parteitage* were primarily designed to present the party to the world – later they became demonstrations of power.

MEMENTOS

Any event with half a million people gathered in one spot is going to leave a powerful impression, and most of those attending the Nazi spectaculars at Nuremberg wanted something personal to remember them by. Ticket stubs and programmes were kept and treasured, while souvenir manufacturers did a brisk trade.

Badges indicating that one had attended one of the Party Days were also valued: they were like the 'pilgrim' badges of the middle ages, showing that the wearer had made the journey to the high temple of Nazidom.

NUREMBERG MEMORIES

Above: Reichsparteitage *were organised to the last detail, and Party souvenirs took a wide variety of forms. The red pennant, bearing the symbol designed for the 1934 rally – each rally had a new design – was produced as a souvenir for cars, though it was also used to adorn bicycles. Some of huge cost of building temporary and permanent facilities at Nuremberg was met by donations from the public: the citation is for a donation of 50 pfennigs collected in Hamburg in 1934. The fine white card would have been attached to a present from the* Oberbürgermeister *or Mayor of Nuremberg. Such gifts would have been presented to important guests.*

Right: Most of the mementos of Party days were cheap items produced by the million. But for the more well-heeled, there was the opportunity to buy high-quality souvenirs from world-renowned manufacturers in the arts and the applied arts. This fine china plate, bearing an image of the medieval centre of Nuremberg and the city arms, also carried the legend 'City of the Reich's Party Days, Nuremberg'. It was manufactured by the famous German porcelain manufacturers at Meissen.

Below: A presentation plaque and case from the 1929 Rally together with a rally badge and a miniature. The 1929 Party Day was important in the development of the party, and the badge became an award of honour.

Above: In Germany as in other countries in the 1930s, no event would be complete without a range of postcards which those who attended could send 'wish you were here' messages to those who stayed home. The Nuremberg rallies attracted a particularly large number of card printers, who produced an incredibly wide range of products. Many of the cards could be bought in Nuremberg all through the year, but others were special editions which were only issued during the week of the Reichsparteitage itself.

Below: The Nazis used the rallies to impress foreign visitors. Here, Rudolf Hess has invited the writer G. Ward Price to the 1939 Party Day – an invitation which had to be foregone when the German invasion of Poland led to Britain's declaration of war.

Above: Each rally generated a vast number of commemorative books and magazines. The most popular were probably the illustrated examples, packed with photographs recording each stage of the event.

Below: In the 1930s, each yearly rally was given its own name, and a special symbol or logo was designed to be used on anything relating to that particular meeting. This rally badge bears the device of the 1937 rally, the 'Reich Congress of Labour', and the device is repeated on the tickets giving entrance to three of the main events of the week-long congress.

Right and below: Party days had not always been held in Nuremberg. The first meeting actually to be called a Parteitage took place at Weimar in 1926: Hitler had been released from prison after the Beerhall putsch but he was still banned from political activity in Bavaria. Beginning on July 3 and ending at noon the following day, it saw the first Blutfahne ceremony (held in secret), and marked the emergence of Joseph Goebbels as a force within the party. Ten years later, the Nazis were in control of Germany. To honour the early Nazis, silver and bronze rally badges were produced to commemorate the first Weimar event. The badge depicted the 'Thüringen' SA standard.

ADOLF HITLER was more than the ruler of Germany: he was the subject of one of the most intense propaganda campaigns in history. It was a campaign which established the Führer's personality cult. There is some evidence that in his early years in power, Hitler looked on the sycophantic effusions of Geobbels' propaganda ministry with some scepticism.

FÜHRER WORSHIP

However, by the late 1930s, fuelled by total power and constant sycophancy, the Führer believed the reality of Goebbels conjured image.

The worship of Adolf Hitler was almost pathological. He was looked on as a man of destiny, even as a demi-god, and his face was everywhere.

FÜHRER MEMENTOS

Most people had a portrait of the Führer or a copy of *Mein Kampf* at the very least. The public were also fed a controlled diet of Hitler images, through newspapers and illustrated magazines. A wide variety of companies made good profits from xeroxing the Führer's face, but items personally associated with the man himself were most valued. Among these were notes and gifts bearing inscriptions or a signature.

The first major change in Hitler's image after coming to power was the need to depict himself as a statesman. Although his normal attire was a military style jacket with plain swastika armband, Hitler was quite prepared to don white tie and tails for diplomatic and other formal functions.

Below: Hitler meets with the British and French foreign ministers in 1934. Such events were widely publicised, usually with the slant that though Hitler was a man of the people, he was also a statesman of the first rank.

HITLER AS ICON

Left: Hitler's 50th Birthday in 1939 was the occasion of a vast amount of official celebration, ranging from military parades and massed party meetings to special dinners, childrens' parties and concerts. A wide array of souvenirs was sold, from kitsch to the extremely expensive. This birthday plaque is one of the latter: made of fine biscuit porcelain, it was manufactured by the old established company of Meissen. It is simple and unadorned, apart from the inscription "Adolf Hitler – our leader – 20 April 1939."

Above: In the Third Reich, anything to do with Adolf Hitler was important. One of the most ubiquitous of all Hitler symbols was Mein Kampf. A copy was owned by almost every Party member and by most German families. Part autobiography and part exposition of Hitler's political and philosophical ideas, it was a turgid read: postwar research has unsurprisingly shown that few of its owners ever managed more than a few pages. Originally published in two volumes in the 1920s, it appeared in a single volume bible-format edition in 1930. This blue leather-bound example is a special edition published in 1939 in honour of the Führer's 50th birthday.

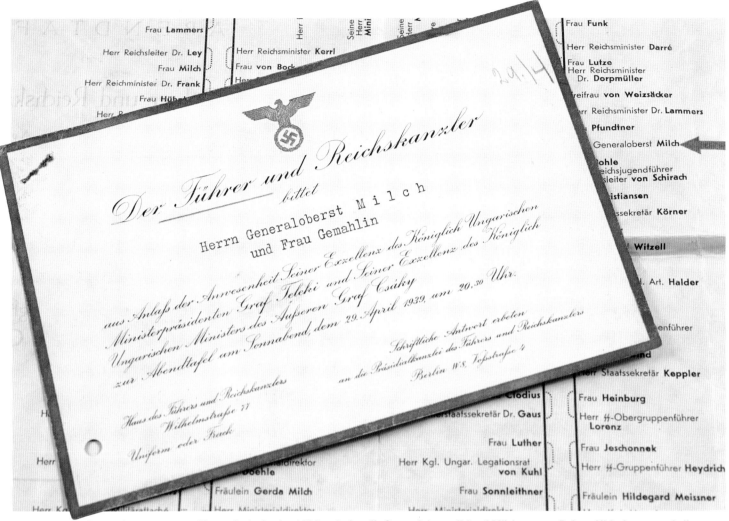

Below: Items of everyday use from the Reichs Chancellery, including a teaspoon with drop-wing eagle/swastika, a bronze visitor's cloakroom tag, and a book of meal tickets, each entitling the bearer to a lunch in the Chancellery canteen.

Above: An invitation bidding Luftwaffe Generaloberst Erhard Milch to attend an evening reception at the Chancellery. The dinner, which took place on 29 April 1939, was in honour of an Hungarian diplomatic mission led by Count Teleki. The request to wear uniform or frack – German for tails – points to the fact that this was to be a formal dinner. The gold-edged card rests on a seating plan which would have been included with the invitation, showing Hitler at the head of the table and with Milch's position indicated by a red arrow.

Below: Hitler's personal silver cutlery, resting on one of the Führer's napkins. There were two main services: the formal service with Grecian border on the handle, used for state dinners, and the simpler informal service for Hitler's everyday use.

BERLIN, Weihnachten 1942

In dankbarer Erinnerung an die schönen Stunden, dank Ihrer künstlerischen Mitwirkung in meinem dorf ich Sie bitten, auch in diesem kleines Weihnachtsgeschenk die mir

Weihnachten 1943

Auch in diesem Jahre bitte ich Sie, in dankbarer Erinnerung an die schönen Stunden, die ich dank Ihrer
künstlerischen Mitwirkung in meinem Hause erleben durfte,
das beifolgende Paket als kleines Weihnachtsgeschenk ent-
gegenzunehmen. Es entstammt wiederum Sendungen, die mir aus
dem Ausland bzw. den besetzten Gebieten zur Verfügung ge-
stellt wurden.

Mit den herzlichsten Glückwünschen für das
Weihnachtsfest und zum Neuen Jahr

Ihr

Below: Hitler hated routine
paperwork, but could not avoid it.
Here he signs a document in the
Reich Chancellery, some time in
the 1930s, watched by SA Staff
Chief Lutze — and by a portrait of
Frederick the Great. Over the years
Hitler's scrawled signature grew
less and less legible.

FROM THE FÜHRER'S DESK

Top: Examples of Adolf Hitler's personal stationery. Until 1942 the letters
were adorned with a gold-block Party Eagle and Swastika, but later
letterheads carried the 'Führer Eagle' which had straight wingtips.
Towards the end of the war only the title was gold-blocked; the national
symbol was blind embossed. With the writing sheets are two pre-printed
cards, also showing the early and late eagles. These cards were used to
reply to letters, or to accompany gifts on special occasions. All bore
Hitler's signature, but very few would ever have been seen by the Führer.
Routine replies carried facsimile signatures. These were of high quality
and looked authentic — most of their recipients (and many post-war
collectors) believed that they had been personally signed by Hitler.

Right: Adolf Hitler's ex libris bookplate used to identify items from
Hitler's personal library. Engraved to a very high standard, his bookplate
carries an example of the 1920 party eagle.

PANZERWAFFE

ALONG WITH the Stuka, the panzer was the defining symbol of National Socialism in its most aggressive form: *Blitzkrieg*. But the terrifying armoured warfare that the panzer represented was not a Nazi creation. It evolved from doctrines created by the German General Staff, embodying tactical lessons learned in the last years of World War I. The *Panzerwaffe* also had traditions rooted firmly in Prussian and Imperial German military history.

PANZER ORIGINS

The first German panzer units were formed in September 1917, but had little impact. Their main legacy to the armoured troops of the Third Reich was the Death's Heads painted on their early tanks, a symbol which would be adopted by the Wehrmacht's *Panzerwaffe*.

Above: The ultimate panzer troops of World War II: the crew of a King Tiger in Budapest in 1945. Although their tank is ten times bigger than those used a decade earlier, their uniforms – apart from their headgear – have changed very little.

Left: An early tank commander stands proud in the turret of his tiny Panzer I. Until 1940/41, the characteristic Basque-style beret was an easy way of recognising panzer troops in the field.

A few tanks were used by *Freikorps* units in the anti-Communist battles of 1919 and 1920, but under the terms of the Versailles treaty the *Reichsheer* was forbidden armour. Tanks would not make a reappearance in German colours until Hitler came to power. However, under the Weimar government the *Reichsheer* had done a considerable amount of theoretical training with motorised and armoured formations, training which was enhanced by practical work carried out at a secret tank school in Kazan, Russia. Motorised units involved in these operations generally wore black leather protective clothing.

NEW *PANZERWAFFE*

The *Reichsheer* began to develop a new uniform for armoured troops in 1929, troop testing taking place in 1932. By the time the first Wehrmacht armoured units were formed in 1934, their members had been issued with the uniform which, with a few changes, was to be worn right up to the end of World War II.

The romantically-inclined claim that the black panzer uniform – protective headgear, combat blouse and trousers – was chosen to incorporate the traditions of the Kaiser's cavalry, particularly the Death's Head Hussars. The choice of Hussar-style swallow-tail regimental flags undoubtedly reinforced the notion, and indeed, tank troops were often called 'The Führer's Black Hussars' in the output of Geobbel's propaganda ministry.

There may have been an element of truth in this view, but the main reason that black clothing was chosen was more likely to have been practical rather than traditional. Tanks are large, messy things, and oil stains are much less obvious on black than on field gray.

The most characteristic item of panzer clothing was the panzer beret. It was worn from 1934 through the early campaigns of the war, and was occasionally seen as late as 1943.

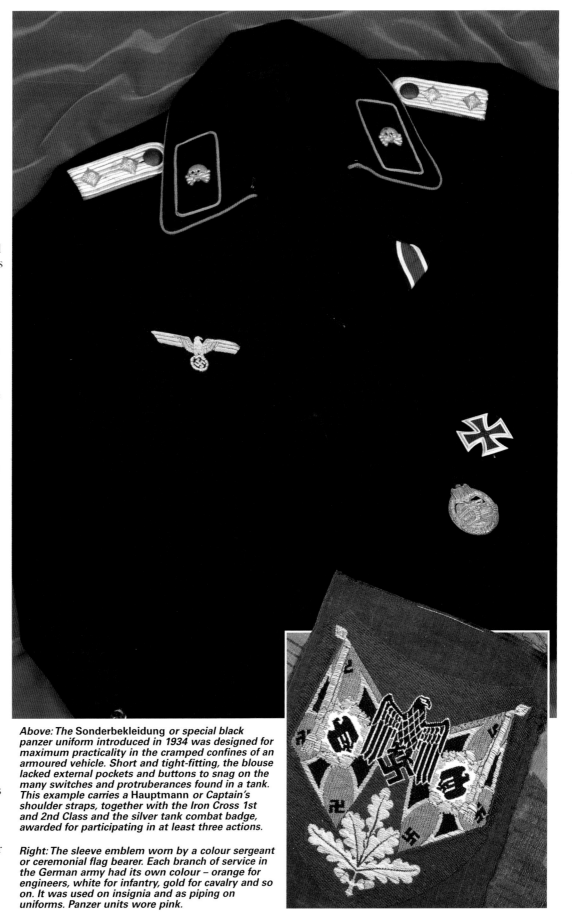

Above: The **Sonderbekleidung** *or special black panzer uniform introduced in 1934 was designed for maximum practicality in the cramped confines of an armoured vehicle. Short and tight-fitting, the blouse lacked external pockets and buttons to snag on the many switches and protruberances found in a tank. This example carries a* **Hauptmann** *or Captain's shoulder straps, together with the Iron Cross 1st and 2nd Class and the silver tank combat badge, awarded for participating in at least three actions.*

Right: The sleeve emblem worn by a colour sergeant or ceremonial flag bearer. Each branch of service in the German army had its own colour – orange for engineers, white for infantry, gold for cavalry and so on. It was used on insignia and as piping on uniforms. Panzer units wore pink.

Above: Hauptmann *Franz,* commander of a battery of assault guns and holder of the Ritterkreuz, sits in his Sturmgeschutz. *Assault gun crews wore panzer-style uniforms in field grey, without the death's head. Since the assault guns were part of the artillery arm, their crews wore red artillery Waffenfarbe.*

Left: Waffen SS tank crews wore army-style panzer uniforms, with arm of service piping on their shoulder straps and the SS-style eagle on the left arm. This expensively tailored jacket was made for an Haupsturmführer or Captain. The decorations include the tank assault badge together with the SA Sports Badge and the German National Sports Badge in bronze. The lack of further combat awards suggests that it dates from early in the war.

Below and below left: Panzer troops wore the distinctive Baskenmutze or Basque beret (below) over a hard rubber padded crash helmet (below left). In 1934 the oakleaf cockade was embroidered direct onto the cloth, but after the introduction of the 'National Eagle' or eagle and swastika, this was replaced by a woven emblem which was sewn on to the beret. SS troops wore similar headgear, but with a large SS eagle and SS-style deaths head.

ARMOURED UNIFORMS

Although armoured troops wore their special panzer uniform operationally, they were also issued with a more conventional uniform. Before the war, the walking out uniform, originally introduced in the 1920s, usually carried *Waffenfarbe* on the epaulettes, around the collar and piping the edges of the coat. In wartime, this was usually replaced by the field jacket: the German army uniform with standard double bars on the collar in place of the *Totenkopf* of the black tunic. This was simpler and less heavily decorated, with panzer pink only appearing on the epaulettes and on the collar bars.

Tank crew and anti-tank units carried pink *Waffenfarbe* all through the war. At the beginning of the conflict, panzergrenadiers also wore pink, but late in the war this was changed to green. Armoured reconnaissance units originally wore cavalry gold, but in the early years of the war they were given their own brown *Waffenfarbe*. From 1943, however, they wore the standard panzer pink.

Top left: The army version of the national eagle and swastika symbol was worn on headgear and on the right breast of the tunic. The triangular cloth version was attached to the peaked Tyrolean-style M43 field cap. The pink-piped death's head collar patch was worn on the black panzer tunic up until the end of the war. The grey-piped epaulette was worn briefly in 1940 by combat engineers attached to panzer units.

Top right: Peaked caps trimmed with appropriate Waffenfarbe were worn by all ranks. Caps for NCOs and enlisted men had a leather cap strap, while officers wore silver metallic cords. This cap has a metal-stamped oakleaf wreath and national symbol as issued: many officers replaced one or both with woven examples.

Right: Items worn by panzer crewmen in the desert. The Afrika Korps cuff title was introduced in July 1941. The brown Tropisches Einheits-feldmütze or tropical field cap is made of hard-wearing cotton drill.

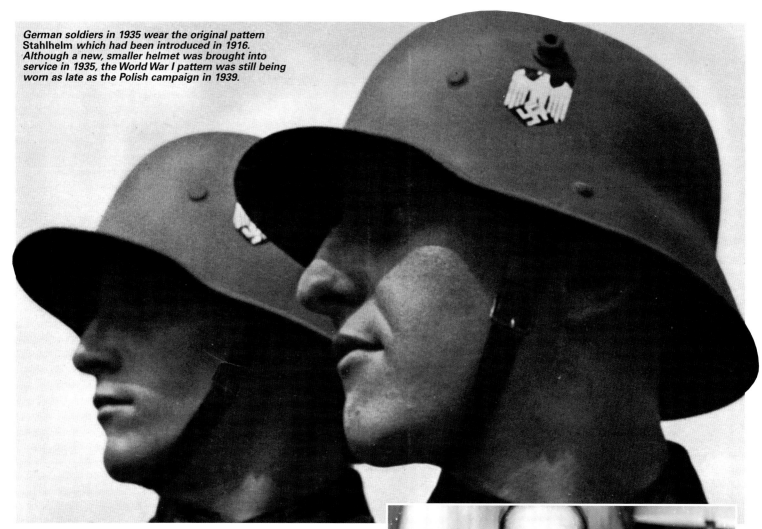

German soldiers in 1935 wear the original pattern Stahlhelm *which had been introduced in 1916. Although a new, smaller helmet was brought into service in 1935, the World War I pattern was still being worn as late as the Polish campaign in 1939.*

GERMAN ARMY

Left: Wehrmacht regimental standards on parade in 1933 for inspection by the new Reichs Chancellor, Adolf Hitler. Although eventually incorporated into the Nazi system, the German army retained much of its Prussian heritage.

Above: Field Marshal Gerd von Rundstedt wears a Reichsheer-style coat, as did many of Hitler's generals. Rundstedt's uniform carries a colonel's insignia, a personal idiosyncrasy on the part of the most senior officer in the German army.

I N 1933, THE German army was little more than a cadre, a 100,000-strong force limited by the Treaty of Versailles and incapable of defending Germany's borders.

On 16 March 1935, Adolf Hitler announced the reintroduction of conscription, and the army began to grow at an astonishing rate.By 1939 Hitler's Wehrmacht had become a formidable war machine, designed to use the newly developed Blitzkrieg tactics to fight and win wars more quickly than any army in history. Its equipment was no better than those of any other army of the time, but its troops were among the best-trained in the world.

NEW UNIFORMS

With the reintroduction of conscription came a whole new series of uniforms. The 1935 patterns were to form the basis for German army field equipment right up to the end of the war, though most were to be modified for ease of manufacture or to save materials under wartime conditions.

The basic field grey uniform (which was in fact a grey-green colour) was standard throughout the army. It consisted of steel helmet, side cap or peaked cap, field tunic and trousers, greatcoat and boots. The jackboots, which were to become symbolic of Nazi conquests, were basically the same pattern as had been worn by Prussian troops in the invasion of France in 1870.

UNIFORM SUPPLIES

In peacetime, the German clothing industry managed to keep pace with the enlargement of the army. Uniforms were smart, reasonably comfortable and practical. However, with the outbreak of war, supply could not meet demand, and conscripts would often find themselves being issued with dyed Czech, Polish or French uniforms to which German insignia and national emblems had been hurriedly applied.

Above: The M1935 pattern tunic was the standard German army field uniform for much of the war. This example was worn by an Unteroffizier (Corporal) of the Grossdeutschland *Regiment who had been awarded the Iron Cross Second Class, the wound badge and the assault badge awarded for supporting at least three infantry or tank assaults. Formed in 1939 from the Army's elite Berlin Guard Regiment,* Grossdeutschland *was to grow to become a Panzer corps in 1944.*

Right: Before the war the 1935 pattern steel helmet or Stahlhelm *generally bore two insignia: on the right the red-white-black shield, and on the left the national symbol of eagle and swastika in silver on a black shield.*

Top left: A Lieutenant General's service tunic. Generals wore red Waffenfarbe, together with gold and silver-plaited shoulder cords and traditional Prussian style collar patches of hand-embroidered gold on red cloth. Although based on the standard German officer's service dress, this tailor-made item has a number of non-standard features – the red piping is more extensive than most, being used on the collar, front panel and on the French cuffs.

Top right: Parade uniform or Waffenrock of an artillery Wachtmeister or Sergeant Major. Introduced in 1935 and based on the uniform of the old Imperial army, this formal dress was discontinued with the outbreak of war – though it was worn as walking out dress by individuals for several years afterwards. Distinguished by its eight-button design and prominent 'Swedish' cuffs, this tunic is trimmed in the bright red Waffenfarbe of the artillery. The owner of this example had been awarded the Iron Cross, an Ostfront campaign medal, the Anschluss medal and the Sudetenland medal. The silver infantry assault badge was awarded for participating in at least three infantry attacks. On the sleeve the Krim shield commemorates taking part in the Crimean campaign of 1941 and 1942, and the oval proficiency badge on the forearm indicates that the bearer was a qualified gun-layer (or aimer of artillery pieces)

Left: A peaked field cap worn by Panzer non-commissioned officers. NCO caps are identifiable from their leather straps and issue aluminium insignia – originally issued in 1935 and worn all through the war. The dress cap was similar, but with wire stiffening.

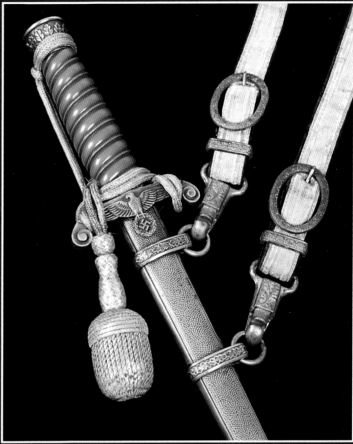

Top left: An officer's field cap and the white Wiffontsha at common service dress, indicating that the wearer was of infantrymen. Also shown are vehicle pennant, a compass and a chronometer.

Top right: The officer's dress dagger was worn pinned with dress uniform or walking out dress of in more elaborate ceremonial occasions. It might be replaced by a sword. This cable-hilt dagger type was approved in May 1942 ... Until December ... it might be carried. After ... it remained an approved item though no longer obtainable ... Unlike swords, which were made to uniform standard designs, the dress daggers generally reflected the tastes of their user.

Below: Jäger, literally "hunter", or light infantry units were marked insignia in the form of oak leaf badges and worn with the cap-badge of infantry. Mountain troops wore an edelweiss flower. Both types of unit were worn worn time.

FELDGRAU OF THE ARMY

The field-grey of the army ... feldgrau grey ... most ... traditional identifying feature of the German soldier ... the colour which permeated the German army throughout the Third Reich ...

SS CUFF TITLES

CUFF TITLES are a traditional uniform item in the German armed forces. Their use dates back to the 19th Century, when they were primarily intended as distinctions for elite units. During World War II, cuff-titles were much more widely applied to the uniforms of many military and paramilitary formations.

Woven tapes, usually between 28mm and 33mm wide, they were worn on the right forearm by the army and the left forearm by the SS. Their purposes were varied: they could identify a wearer's function, or in which geographical area his unit was raised. In the fighting services, however, they were primarily used to identify a military unit, though they were also used as campaign awards. As unit identifiers, they could carry the unit's name or number, or they could be used to commemorate military heroes or Nazi 'martyrs.'

Cuff titles were widely used by the SS. Most pre-war units had them – they were issued to members on joining, along with their uniforms. Initially all were hand embroidered with aluminium wire, but from 1936 this quality was reserved for officers. Other ranks were issued with tapes that were machine-embroidered in cotton. This was the so-called RZM pattern.

WARTIME ECONOMIES

From 1939, gothic lettering was abandoned. Officers' titles were machine-woven rather than hand-embroidered, though metallic thread was still used for the lettering. From 1943, however, with the war turning against Germany even that was too expensive, and all ranks were issued with woven cloth titles. Known as the 'BEVO' pattern after the trademark of the principle manufacturer of such tapes, they were worn to the end of the war.

Any SS man moving from one unit to another had to switch cuff titles – unless his new unit had not been awarded such an honour. In that case, he could continue to wear the title of his old unit.

Opposite page: Obergruppenführer Joseph 'Sepp' Dietrich collects for the Winterhilfe charity soon after the Nazi seizure of power. His black SS uniform is adorned with the 'Adolf Hitler' cuff title, worn only by Hitler's bodyguard, the Leibstandarte-SS Adolf Hitler

Top inset: Early cuff titles were embroidered in gothic lettering, though late in 1939 these were replaced by latin letters. These examples were worn by staff and students at the two SS officer training schools. The wire-woven Bad Tölz band was worn by officers, while the Braunschweig title is in the cotton-embroidered 'RZM' style used by NCOs and other ranks.

Above inset: Most SS cuff titles were black with white, silver or grey lettering. This unique green and white example was manufactured in October 1944 for use by the 1st Musselmann (Muslim) Regiment, comprised of volunteers from Turkestan. It is unlikely that these cuff titles were ever issued to the members of the regiment.

Main picture: Greatcoat worn by an Unterscharführer (corporal) of the third armed SS regiment, Der Führer. In 1940 this became a part of the SS-VT Division, along with the Deutschland and Germania regiments. Regimental cuff titles were still worn even after the division was renamed Das Reich and a divisional cuff title was introduced in 1942.

Above: Heinrich Himmler is seen making a triumphal progress through the occupied territories of Eastern Europe early in the war. As the head of the SS, he can be regarded as the highest of all 'Main SS Office' chiefs, and he wears the black and silver Hauptamtchef cuff title. Only 12 other men could wear it.

Below: Karl Hermann Frank, Minister of State in Bohemia and Moravia. A Sudeten German, he succeeded the assassinated Reinhard Heydrich as acting Protector, and took a terrible revenge on the village of Lidice. One step below the main office holders, he wears the Reichsführung-SS cuff title.

Below: The Hauptamtchef cuffband of silver woven brocade with black stripes was one of the rarest of all such items. They were worn only by the heads of main SS offices – the 12 department heads appointed by and answerable to Reichsführer SS Heinrich Himmler. Included among their number were Karl Wolff, Reinhard Heydrich, Ernst Kaltenbrunner, Kurt Daluege, August Heissmeyer and Oswald Pohl. Wolff was head of the the Reichsführer's personal staff, and staff members wore the Reichsführung-SS cuffband, also worn by members of the SS high command. The runic 'SS' was adopted in September 1939 – before that date the letters were written in a gothic script.

Above: The 3rd SS-Division Totenkopf was built around a nucleus of former concentration camp guards. The Totenkopf was commanded by Theodor Eicke, who was killed in Russia in 1942. His name was awarded to SS-Panzergrenadier Regiment 6.

Below: The Freiwillige (foreign volunteer) Legions Flandern and Niederlande both earned fighting reputations on the Eastern front, but suffered grievously, almost being wiped out on several occasions. They were disbanded in 1943. The Dutch cuff band is machine embroidered in the RZM style, while the Flemish band is BEVO woven.

Below: Embroidered Allgemeine SS officer's titles, indicating that the wearers served with SS Standarte 3, from Nuremberg; Standarte 6 at Berlin-Charlottenburg; Standarte 9 from Hannover, and Standarte 72 based in Detmold.

Above: In the 1930s, coloured borders were used to indicate which Sturmbann or company of an Allgemeine SS Standarte a man belonged to. Light blue indicated the reserve: green, dark blue and red indicated Sturmbanns I, II and III respectively. The wheel indicates an early motorised unit.

Below left: SS Regiment Deutschland became part of the SS-VT division in 1940. Before the war the regimental cuff title was in gothic script, changed to latin letters in 1939. Seen here are examples of officer's titles hand-woven in wire above the 'RZM' embroidered titles worn by NCOs and other ranks. RZM stood for Reichszugmeisterei, and indicated material made to the order of the Nazi party contracts office.

Below: The 11th SS Mountain regiment was awarded the Heydrich name after the latter's assassination in 1942. Beneath that is a pre-war, silver bullion title awarded to SS-Standarte II 'Wien'. Planetta was an Austrian Nazi killed in the abortive coup of 1934. Artur Phleps was the commander of the Prinz Eugen division, killed in 1944. The title was awarded to the 13th volunteer mountain regiment, but was never issued. It is in the machine-woven BEVO style (after the Wuppertal firm of Bandfabrik Ewald Vorsteher, the largest manufacturer of such items).

MEMORIALS AND HONOURS

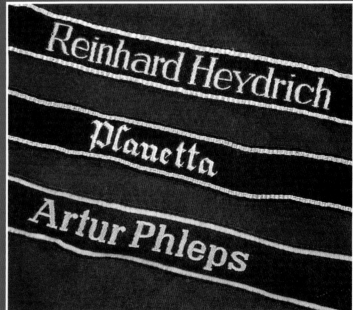

INFANTRY
EQUIPMENT

AN INFANTRY soldier spends most of his time on his feet. He cannot rely on supply trains or baggage wagons, so he must carry everything he needs for combat and basic survival on his person. From Roman times, the foot soldier has marched with heavy loads, and a large part of any field uniform is designed to enable him to sling those loads in the most comfortable – or perhaps more accurately the least uncomfortable – fashion.

MAJOR LOAD

First, he must have his fighting gear: his rifle, ammunition, a bayonet or knife, an entrenching tool, grenades and perhaps a gas mask. To fight with those weapons he needs to be fit, so the second priority is water, rations and first-aid supplies. On top of that he must also carry equipment relevant to his role – radios for communications specialists, extra ammunition for machine gun crews, tools for engineers. And because he has to be able to fight in all weathers, he needs blankets, greatcoats and poncho/tent sections.

In the German army all this was secured by a complex harness of leather – tough and strong, capable of being buffed to a brilliant shine for parades, but not ideal for some climactic conditions. It was not until late in the war that more modern webbing material found its way to the front line.

Left: A much decorated **Unteroffizier** *of the infantry poses with friends after having been awarded the Knight's Cross. He is clothed and equipped in early war style, and on his leather belt and combat straps he is carrying a pistol, binoculars, a map case and a compass.*

Right: A near complete set of German infantry equipment, left behind in a barn when a wounded SS man was evacuated from Normandy in 1944. An Army infantryman would have carried virtually identical gear, with the exception of the SS camouflage clothing.

Above left: The German Army"s standard 80-cl M31 Feldflasche *– Field Flask or water bottle – was made from aluminium, with a felt covering for insulation. It came with a cup which was usually painted black, and which was carried strapped over the screw cap. The Afrika Korps version, for use under the fierce desert sun, was made of plastic-impregnated wood, with a bakelite cup.*

Above: The S84/98 bayonet was used on the German Army's Gewehr 98 rifles. Turning a rifle into a spear is normally of little practical use, but the bayonet was a fearsome close-quarters weapon in the bitter fighting on the Eastern Front. The metal scabbard was hung from a leather frog, which had a hilt-retaining strap added during the war. The frog looped through the field belt – this is an SS example – and the bayonet was worn on the left hip.

Left: The classic German jackboot began to be replaced early in the war by conventional lace-up boots, which used less leather in their construction. These high-quality brown leather mountain boots were issued to Gebirgsjäger, who needed the heavy studs and cleats for grip in snow and ice. The experimental canvas 'Styrian' gaiters were issued for trials with the SS-Gebirgs-Division Nord.

Left: The Tornister or pack was made from canvas, though the flap was covered in horse- or cow-hide. The original M34 pattern had integral straps, but the M39 version seen here attached direct to the combat 'Y' straps or braces. It was usually kept with the baggage train in combat. Until the outbreak of war the M35 helmet was polished, but wartime examples were issued in a matt finish in various shades of grey. In the field soldiers would often roughen the finish further.

Below left: A pair of Model 1911 black grained leather ammunition pouches for the K98 Mauser rifle. These examples were issued to the SS, as they carry SS/RZM stamps and serial numbers .

Below: The M35 map case used by most of the German armed forces. This example in brown leather was carried by a Luftwaffe signals officer. It had three main compartments for holding maps and charts, notebooks, and scale rulers and protractors. Pencils, pens and writing equipment had their own holders on the front flap. Compasses were often carried on a lanyard.

FIELD GEAR

Nuremberg, on 10 September 1934. Reichsarbeitsführer Konstantin Hierl watches as 50,000 members of the Reichs Labour service parade in front of their Führer. Hierl, a former army colonel, wears his World War I decorations on his RAD uniform. The golden spade on his arm shield was only worn by Hierl and senior members of the Reich leadership of the RAD.

REICH LABOUR SERVICE

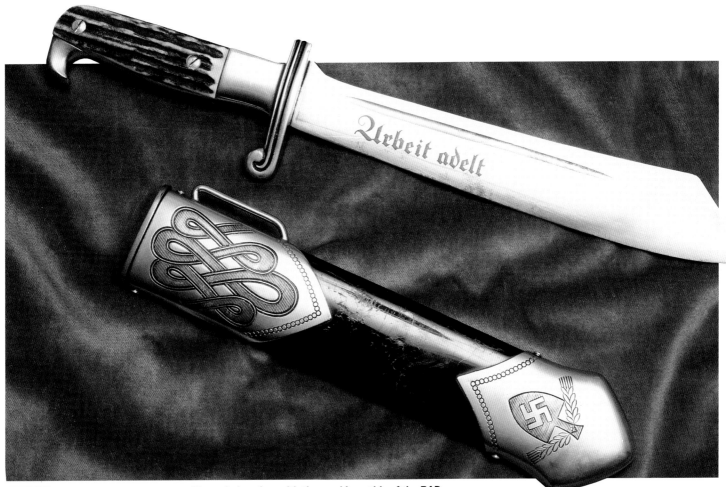

Above: In keeping with the working ethic of the RAD, the organisation's official blade arm was an axe-like 'hewer' rather than a dagger or a sword. The non-commissioned version seen here had staghorn grips: the officer's version was slimmer, with a more stylised eagle's head top and ivorine hand grip plates.

Below: A photo album of the type sold in the canteens of all German services. Generally well-made, they carried the symbol of the particular service embossed on their covers. This RAD album was owned by a female member, and is shown with

THE ORIGINS of the Nazi labour service date back to 1931, when the Weimar government established the *Freiwilliger Arbeitsdienst* or Volunteer labour service. It was designed to provide national coordination for the large number of local work projects established to fight unemployment in the late 1920s. Nazi Party member Konstantin Hierl became head of the new organisation.

NAZIFICATION

In 1933 the organisation was renamed the National Socialist labour service or NSAD, becoming the more familiar RAD or *Reichsarbeitsdienst* a year later. In 1935, a six months service with the RAD became compulsory for all males between the ages of 18 and 25. Before the war the RAD took part in large scale labour projects: once war broke out its primary function was to provide the Wehrmacht with logistics and construction support.

Above: An epaulette denoting the rank of Reichsarbeitsführer, *worn only by the head of the* Reichsarbeitsdienst, *Konstantin Hierl. Hierl was a former Staff Colonel and Freikorps member who had been a follower of Ludendorff during the Munich Putsch. He joined the Nazi Party in 1927, becoming a party official in 1929. He was appointed* Reichsarbeitsführer *in 1935 when labour service became compulsory. The epaulette is one of the Third Pattern insignia, introduced in 1942. The collar patch was worn only by Hierl and the* Generalarbeitsführer. Arbeitsführer *wore the same pattern patch in silver.*

Above: The Reichsarbeitsdienst *was divided into 40* Arbeitsgau, *or divisional districts, identified by Roman numerals. Each* Arbeitsgau *controlled about eight battalion-sized units called* Arbeitsgruppen. *These sleeve shields were worn by female leaders in* Arbeitsgau IX, *which covered Brandenburg West, and* Arbeitsgau XVIII, *which administered Niedersachsen-Ost. Beneath is a basic silvered RAD membership brooch.*

In common with most German uniformed organisations, when travelling by car senior officers would have their vehicle adorned with an identifying pennant. Officers entitled to use this ornate Reichsarbeitsdienst *car pennant included* Arbeitsdienst Inspekteure, *(Labour Inspectors),* Arbeitsgauführer *(RAD District Leader) and* Amtschef *(Departmental heads).*

WORKING FOR THE FÜHRER

Above: The Reichsarbeitsdienst wore a characteristic forester's or 'Robin Hood' cap. As with most German uniforms of the period, the colour of the piping was significant. The silver piping indicates that this was worn by an officer: general's caps were trimmed in gold, while those of NCOs and other ranks carried black trim. The collar patch and epaulettes were worn by an Arbeitsführer.

Left: The spade and wheat insignia signified the RAD's affinity with labour and the land. The sports vest shield was worn on the chest. It is seen with the aluminium cap badge worn by NCOs and other ranks (and occasionally by officers), a cloth cap badge worn by other ranks, and the lower-sleeve shield bearing the 'life' rune which was worn by medical personnel.

Far left: The 'TS' sleeve shield indicates that the bearer was on the staff of a Truppenführerschule or officer training school. The other arm shield was worn by NCOs attached to the 6th Abteilung of Arbeitsgruppe 76 – part of Arbeitsgau VII in Schleswig-Holstein. The woven aluminium cap badge was used by officers.

The fiercely-independent Cossacks chafed under the rule of Moscow. Large numbers fought on the German side, under the command of General Andrej Vlassov. Most started out in the Wehrmacht, but in November 1944 the SS took over, with the aim of creating a Cossack Cavalry Corps – two full divisions.

FOREIGN LEGIONS

EW PEOPLE realise just how international the German forces in World War II were. It is estimated that nearly two million foreign nationals served under the swastika. Many were volunteers, but a large number were more or less willing conscripts. In 1944, a report to *Reichsführer* SS Heinrich Himmler recorded that there were more than 800,000 former Soviet citizens serving with the Wehrmacht and the Waffen-SS, with a further 100,000 in Luftwaffe or Kriegsmarine Uniform. Many of these men were not so much fighting for the Germans as fighting against Stalin, while others chose the German flag as a more attractive alternative to the brutality of a prison camp.

ANTI-COMMUNISTS

There were also hundreds of thousands of volunteers from the west. They too were keen to join the crusade against Bolshevism, but their motivations were somewhat different. Eastern volunteers had direct experience of living under Soviet rule. The young men from countries like Holland, France, Spain and Norway joined the fight out of conviction, right-wing idealists

who wanted to halt the seemingly inexorable advance of Marxism.

Few of the early volunteers stayed beyond their initial two-year contract with the Germans, but those who did continue to fight did so to the end, many giving their lives in the defence of Berlin in 1945.

Above: The maroon red fez, collar patch and arm shield worn by the 13th Waffen-Gebirgs Division Der SS 'Handschar' (Kroatisches Nr 1). The word Handschar *is Turkish for scimitar, and the unit symbol included such a sword. Raised in 1943 from Bosnian Muslims for use in anti-partisan operations, the division had a poor record – its Muslim troops mutinied in training, killing several of their German cadre members.*

Below: Heinrich Himmler believed that Muslims would make good shock troops, and persisted in his attempts to create an Islamic SS unit. The Osttürkischer Waffenverband der SS was composed of former Soviet Muslims from Turkestan who had come over to the Germans. It was given its own collar patch and unique cuffband, but they were made too late to reach the troops before the end of the war.

Above: Formed in April 1944 largely from Albanian and Kossovo Muslim volunteers, the 21st Waffen-Gebirgs Division SS Skanderbeg *was not a top line unit. Considered to be fit only for security missions, it was hampered by the fact that many of its Muslim troops were more interested in settling scores with Serbs than in fighting for Hitler and the Reich.*

Below: Arm and collar patch for SS-Panzergrenadier Regiment 24 Danmark, part of the 11th SS-Panzergrenadier Division Nordland. *The first Danish unit to carry the national flag as an arm patch was the* Freikorps Danmark, *formed in 1940 and disbanded after hard service in 1943. Survivors formed the nucleus of the new regiment, which wore a curved swastika as a collar patch.*

Above: Early Dutch volunteers served in the Freiwilligen Legion Niederland, *formed in 1941. The Legion was disbanded in 1943, and the* SS-Freiwilligen Brigade Nederland *was established. This was later given Panzergrenadier division status. The collar patch carried what was known as a 'Wolf's Hook' device, while the arm shield was in the colours of the Dutch national flag.*

Below: Volunteers from Flanders originally served in the Freiwilligen Legion Flandern, *whose collar patch was the three-legged swastika known as a Trifos. Disbanded in 1943, some members of the unit were assigned to the* Das Reich *infantry regiment* Langemarck, *which was combined with a Finnish regiment to form a brigade, later expanded into a division. It was all but wiped out at the end of 1944.*

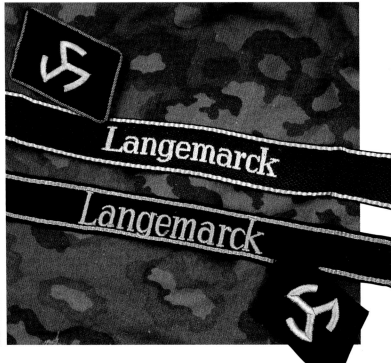

Left: A number of Italian Fascists resolved to continue the war after the Italian surrender in 1943. The Legion Italia fought in Italy, distinguishing itself in the fighting around Anzio. Until that time Himmler refused to allow them to join the SS proper, and the unit insignia had a red background. After Anzio, however, some regiments were accepted into the Waffen SS and were allowed to wear black SS patches. Seen here is a late-war group comprising officers and NCO/other rank collar patches and an armshield. By the end of the war the unit had become the 29th Waffen-Grenadier Division der SS (Italienische Nr. 1).

Below: Although the Germans had established Latvian police units almost as soon as they invaded, it was not until March 1943 that they asked for volunteers for a fighting unit. 32,000 Latvians responded, and the 15th Waffen-Grenadier Division der SS (Lettische Nr.1) was formed. Many of the division's members wore standard SS runes on their collars, but in 1944 a new 'Sun and Stars' pattern was introduced. The division was forced out of Latvia by the advancing Red Army, and surrendered to the British in 1945.

ARMY or SS?

THE BULK of the early volunteers fighting for Hitler served with the German Army. Those from Eastern Europe were initially used in secondary roles, serving in police battalions or as prison camp guards, working as labourers or moving supplies on the long lines of communication. But gradually, as the pressure on German manpower increased, they were used more and more often as combat troops. Some fought extremely well, while others were worthless in battle. Some of the auxiliary units, particularly those employed by the *Einsatzgruppen* and as camp and ghetto guards were among the worst perpetrators of war crimes.

Many western volunteers also served with the army, some in large enough numbers to field divisional-sized formations. However, large numbers also joined the Waffen-SS. Himmler, limited by the army on the number of men he could recruit from the German population, looked to the 'Nordic' countries of occupied Europe to make up the difference. Later, as manpower demands grew apace with Himmler's ambitions, SS racial standards were relaxed and units were formed from Muslims, Slavs, Indians and other asiatics. Some of these units fought well, but most were of poor quality.

A personally-dedicated photograph of Arthur Seyss-Inquart, a leading Austrian Nazi who gained notoriety as the Reich governor of the Netherlands between 1942 and 1945.

SCHUTZSTAFFEL PERSONALITIES

PERSONAL ITEMS with SS connections are among the most sought-after by collectors of militaria. A surprising amount survived the war – though a vastly greater quantity of forgeries and reproductions make the business of collecting such items something of a minefield.

Sources for such material vary. A great deal found its way into the hands of the Allied soldiers who occupied Germany at the end of the war, often gathering dust in lofts and cellars until sold many years later. A smaller amount reached the market from the original owners or recipients of awards – those who survived the war crimes trials and de-Nazification processes of the 1940s and 1950s, and who needed ready cash. More came from members of their families.

MAJOR LOAD

High demand and high prices make collecting SS memorabilia a task which should not be undertaken lightly. Knowledge is vital, whether gained from years of handling such items or from extensive research – though even the most knowledgeable of collectors can occasionally get taken in. Good reference material makes the task easier, and as with all antique collecting a believable and verified provenance provides the best security, as does dealing with reputable suppliers.

Above right: The unique collar patch worn by Heinrich Himmler as Reichsführer-SS. He adopted the design in 1934 after the final separation of the SA and the SS, and it continued unchanged until the end of the Third Reich.

Right: A Parade medal set worn by SS-Obergruppenführer August Frank, one of the few items left in his possession after his home was searched for war booty by American soldiers. Frank was a former police president who became a close associate of SS industrial overlord Oswald Pohl.

Above: The SS 'leader' Ausweis or identity card of SS-Oberführer Benno Martin. Martin, who was to rise to the rank of Obergruppenführer, was Höhere SS und Polizei Führer at Nuremberg between 1941 and the end of the war. The Pope was a character witness at Martin's war crimes trial, saying that the senior SS officer had saved Nuremberg cathedral from destruction.

Below: Knight's Cross of the War Merit Cross with swords, awarded to SS-Obergruppenführer Oswald Pohl, head of the SS economics organisation. Pohl lost his medals when in custody after the war. They were acquired by the warden of the jail in which he was imprisoned, Richard G. Raabe. These and many other such items were kept by Raabe until 1991, when he sold them. The sale, which included a similar Knight's Cross awarded to SS-Obergruppenführer Gottlob Berger, aroused great interest among collectors of Nazi memorabilia.

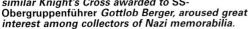

Above: Tailored, open-necked tunic which once belonged to Obergruppenführer Oswald Pohl. Many of Pohl's uniforms survived the war, being kept by his wife who sold them to a local theatrical company. This example was acquired in the 1950s by military historian Andrew Mollo. The tunic bears the Party Badge in Gold, the SA Sports Badge in Bronze, and the Iron Cross First Class from the First World War.

Left: Collar patch and epaulet for the rank of SS-Obergruppenführer belonging to Reichsleiter Martin Bormann. Although strictly a Party official, Bormann was one of the most influential men in Hitler's immediate circle, and was given high SS rank. These examples were taken by occupying American troops from a white summer uniform Bormann had left in his house on the Obersalzberg.

Left: The Golden Party Badge and Citation belonging to SS-Obergruppenführer Karl Freiherr von Eberstein, a long-time associate of Himmler's. Eberstein was Höhere SS und Polizei Führer Süd in Munich from April 1938 until the last months of the war. On the orders of Martin Bormann he was dismissed from his post in February 1945, charged with defeatism.

Above: Eberstein had served as an artilleryman during the First World War. This group of mementoes of his army service includes epaulets from both the 17th and 75th Field Artillery regiments, together with two of his pocket diaries and a personalised clothing name tag. Eberstein was a family friend of the Heydrichs, and introduced Reinhard Heydrich to Himmler.

MEMORIES OF SERVICE

Below: This hand-made parchment presentation folder was given to SS-Standartenführer Henning von Nordeck by his personal staff in 1936. Nordeck was commander of the 1st SS-Motorstandarte or regiment. Motorstandarte were units of the Allgemeine-SS rather than the armed units which were to become the Waffen-SS. Nordeck later joined the Luftwaffe and rose to the rank of Oberstleutnant.

Below: Once the NSDAP came to power, senior Nazis like von Eberstein were treated in much the same way that aristocrats had been in days gone by. Eberstein even had a march composed in his honour. It was written by Gustav Adolf Bunge, Professor of Music in Munich and Director of Music for the SS-Standarte Deutschland. The unit was eventually to become part of the Das Reich Division.

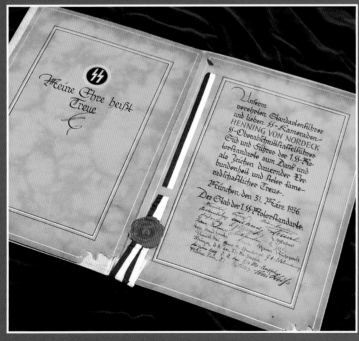

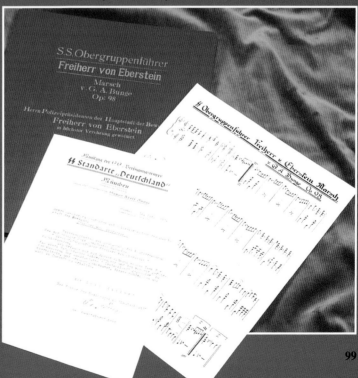

PARTY ART

The 'Germania Soldier' bust was created in the 1930s in the classical head and shoulders style. The helmet depicted is the M1916 pattern introduced by the Imperial German Army halfway through the Great War, which was used by the Reichswehr and the Wehrmacht into the late 1930s. Casts of such busts came in a variety of sizes, and were often given as presentation pieces with suitable dedication plaques fitted to marble bases.

The Eagle and Swastika were amongst the most common of all Nazi symbols. The eagle with 'drop' wings was used massively at the Nuremberg rally ground, and the design was replicated for use as desk or mantlepiece ornaments to commemorate the various Parteitage. The example below, measuring 22 cm in height, was finished in silver plate. The presentation plaque shows that it was given as a trophy by SA-Gruppe Franken, which included Nuremberg in its territory. The smaller than usual eagle to the left is 15-cm high. It had a bronze patina applied during manufacture, and is typical of the kind of ornament which could be bought from NSDAP-controlled shops in Nuremberg.

ART IN THE Nazi state was strictly controlled. Hitler was the ultimate arbiter of what was acceptable, and his tastes ran strongly in the direction of the realistic and the heroic. While other senior Nazis such as Goering and Goebbels might have had more eclectic tastes, in public at least they followed the party line.

SCULPTURE

Sculpture was perhaps the most characteristic of all the Nazi arts, favouring realistic portraiture and works on a monumental scale. Well-off Germans could acquire reproductions of the massive works made by Arno Breker or Josef Thorak, as well as scaled down copies of notable Nazi monuments and symbols.

One exception to the 'realistic' rule was the kind of folk-art inspired by Himmler and the SS. Pieces, often carved from wood, were acceptable if they harked back to an earlier time or could be demonstrated to be *Volkisch* or made in a traditional German style.

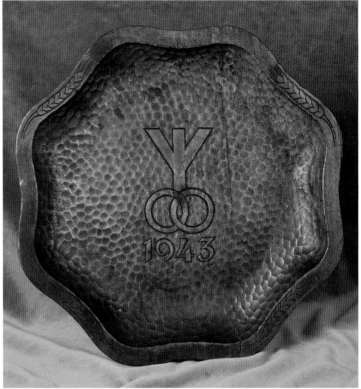

Above: A carved 'wedding' plate was a treasured memento of German marriage ceremonies. Traditionally bread would be eaten from such plates at anniversaries and other festive occasions through the year. This example has ears of wheat, a traditional fertility symbol, carved into the rim, together with interlocking wedding rings and a 'life' rune above the year of marriage – 1943 in this case.

Above left: Carved wooden ornaments have always been popular in rural areas of Germany. The Nazis, with their 'back to the land' philosophy, saw them as ideal gifts. This plate was presented to the commander of the 27th SS Freiwillige Grenadier Division Langemarck *for the winter solstice or* Yulfest *in 1944 – just days before the understrength unit was thrown into the fighting in East Prussia. The division's symbol was a Trifos or three-legged sunwheel swastika, and the example at the centre of this plate was mirrored by three carved horse heads.*

Left: A replica of the massive bronze plaque erected by the Nazis beside Munich's Feldherrenhalle. Located where Residenzstrasse entered the Odeonsplatz, the monument commemorated the 16 Nazis who were killed during the abortive Putsch on 9 November 1923. The monument played a major part in the Nazi celebration of the Putsch, and desk replicas like this were sold in a number of Munich art shops.

Adolf Hitler's image was omnipresent in Germany during the Third Reich. Busts were a popular if expensive way of honouring the Nazi Führer, and many different examples were executed by sculptors all over the Reich. They varied from small to very large. Some were one-off works of art produced to special commission. Others were expensive limited edition bronzes. This example, by Otto Schmidt-Hofer, has a dark green patina applied to spelter (zinc alloy). Lower quality copies were mass-produced and sold through commercial outlets.

NAZI DAGGERS

EDGED WEAPONS were omnipresent in the Third Reich. Knives, daggers, swords, hewers and bayonets were part of the dress uniform of virtually every organisation in the Nazi state, from the armed services to the Hitler Youth. Daggers were key items in the regalia of the SS and the SA, but they were also worn by organisations as diverse as the German Red Cross, the Diplomatic Service, the Forestry Service, the National Political Education Institute and Railway, Customs and Postal officials.

HONOUR SYMBOL

Daggers meant different things to different organisations. For the army, navy and air force, they were the symbol of the warrior, and were often worn in the place of dress swords. For the Stormtroopers of the SA, daggers were simply part of the uniform and were issued in huge numbers.

To the SS, however, daggers were especially significant. An SS-*Mann* was only entitled to wear his dagger after graduating from probationary SS-*Anwärter*. They were presented as part of the ceremony which took place only on 9 November, the anniversary of the Munich Putsch. Each SS member had to pay for his own dagger, and those dismissed from the organisation had to return the weapon to one of the three main Uniform centres at Munich, Berlin or Dresden.

Left: Members of the Nationalsozialistische Kraftfahr-Korps, the NSKK, look on as Adolf Hitler consecrates Deutschland Erwache banners at Nuremberg. Like the SS, the NSKK was originally part of the SA, which is why its uniform dagger is of the SA pattern.

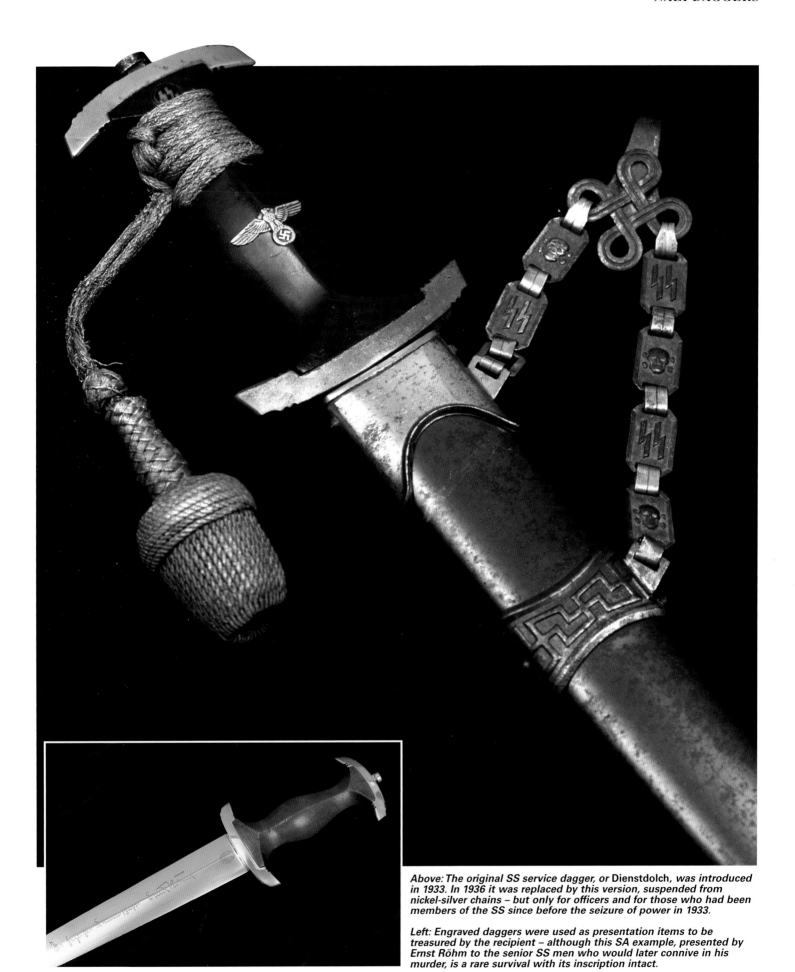

Above: The original SS service dagger, or Dienstdolch, was introduced in 1933. In 1936 it was replaced by this version, suspended from nickel-silver chains – but only for officers and for those who had been members of the SS since before the seizure of power in 1933.

Left: Engraved daggers were used as presentation items to be treasured by the recipient – although this SA example, presented by Ernst Röhm to the senior SS men who would later connive in his murder, is a rare survival with its inscription intact.

Left: The workmanlike dagger worn by junior ranks in the German Red Cross, recognisable by its saw-tooth blade. The grips were of hard-wearing Bakelite.

Below: An early 'second pattern' Luftwaffe dagger made by Alcoso. The celluloid grip varied in colour from the orange/brown seen here to pale yellow.

Above: Policemen did not carry a dagger, being issued a dress bayonet instead. This example, made by the Solingen firm of Alcoso, has a standard staghorn grip and nickel-plated fittings.

Right: The brass scabbard and hilt fittings of this naval officer's dagger are lavishly gilded, as are the scabbard suspension bands which attached the weapon to the uniform belt.

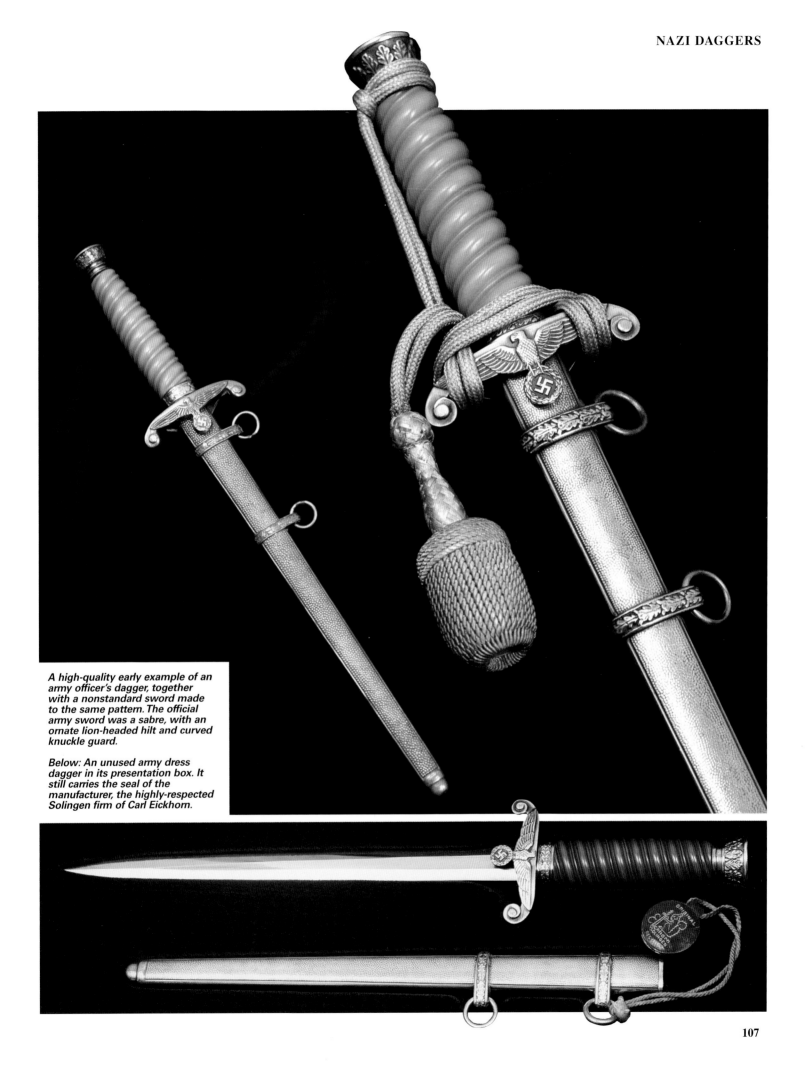

A high-quality early example of an army officer's dagger, together with a nonstandard sword made to the same pattern. The official army sword was a sabre, with an ornate lion-headed hilt and curved knuckle guard.

Below: An unused army dress dagger in its presentation box. It still carries the seal of the manufacturer, the highly-respected Solingen firm of Carl Eickhorn.

NAZI EDUCATION

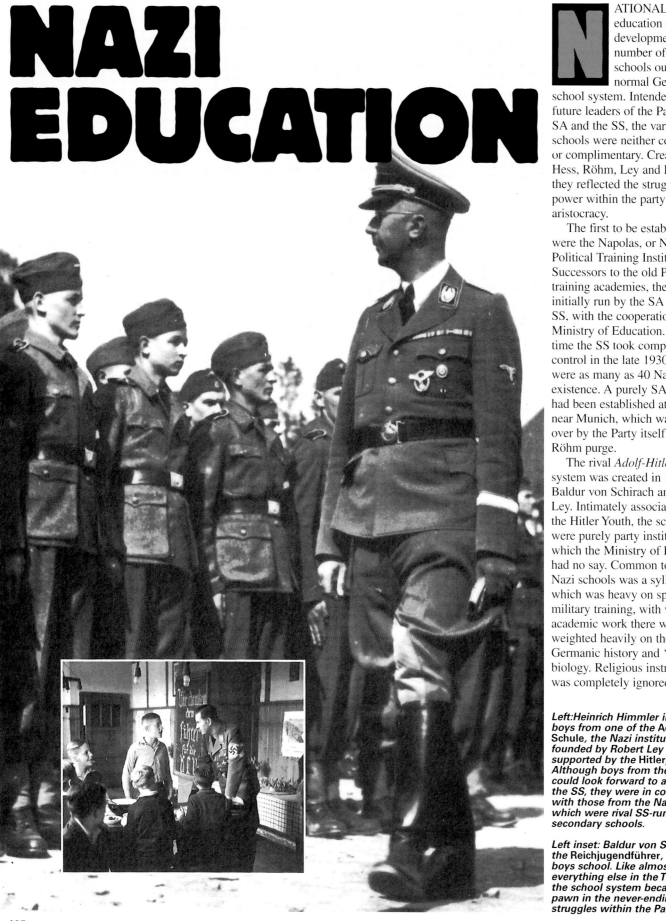

NATIONAL Socialist education saw the development of a number of party schools outside the normal German school system. Intended to foster future leaders of the Party, the SA and the SS, the various schools were neither coordinated or complimentary. Created by Hess, Röhm, Ley and Himmler, they reflected the struggle for power within the party aristocracy.

The first to be established were the Napolas, or National Political Training Institutes. Successors to the old Prussian training academies, they were initially run by the SA and the SS, with the cooperation of the Ministry of Education. By the time the SS took complete control in the late 1930s, there were as many as 40 Napolas in existence. A purely SA school had been established at Feldafing near Munich, which was taken over by the Party itself after the Röhm purge.

The rival *Adolf-Hitler-Schule* system was created in 1936 by Baldur von Schirach and Robert Ley. Intimately associated with the Hitler Youth, the schools were purely party institutions, in which the Ministry of Education had no say. Common to all of the Nazi schools was a syllabus which was heavy on sports and military training, with what academic work there was being weighted heavily on the side of Germanic history and 'Aryan' biology. Religious instruction was completely ignored.

*Left:Heinrich Himmler inspects boys from one of the **Adolf Hitler Schule**, the Nazi institutions founded by Robert Ley and supported by the **Hitlerjugend**. Although boys from the schools could look forward to a place in the SS, they were in competition with those from the Napolas, which were rival SS-run Nazi secondary schools.*

*Left inset: Baldur von Schirach, the **Reichjugendführer**, visits a boys school. Like almost everything else in the Third Reich, the school system became a pawn in the never-ending power struggles within the Party.*

A Party tunic belonging to a candidate member of Krössinsee, one of the three Ordensburgen or 'Order Castles' where future Reich leaders were taught. Krössinsee was in Pomerania (now part of Poland). The two other Ordensburgen were Sonthofen, in the Bavarian Alps, and Vogelsang in Nordrhein-Westfalen.

REICHSSCHULE DER NSDAP. FELDAFING

BEURTEILUNG

ÜBER DEN JUNGMANN   Klaus Fobke

DER 5a   KLASSE AUS   Stuttgart-Sonnenberg

GAU   Württemberg-Hohenzollern.

I KÖRPERLICHE VERANLAGUNG UND SPORTLICHE LEISTUNGEN

Wenig gewachsen, leistungsmäßig aber gut ent...
Gewandt, flink, hart, im Spiel überlegt und ...

II CHARAKTER UND PERSÖNLICHKEIT:

Fobke ist in Haltung und Führung ausge...
worden, ohne seine Lebhaftigkeit und Frisch...
verlieren, doch fehlen ihm noch ausgeprägte ...
kraft und kritische Selbstzucht.

Above: A Ski-style cap or Einheitzmütze worn by a candidate at an Ordensburg, used from 1939 through the early years of the war. Candidates spent a year at each of the facilities, and since Sonthofen in the Alps specialised in ski and mountain training, this cap was probably issued there.

Above left: A peaked visor cap belonging to a candidate at one of the Ordensburgen, probably issued just before the war. Similar in style to those worn by Hitler Youth Leaders, it carries a 'Party'-style Eagle and a plain national cockade. It lacks the gold leaves around the cockade which members of the Party Leadership Corps wore.

Left: A school report from the Reichsschule der NSDAP, located at Feldafing, together with an identity card issued by the NSDAP Oberschule at Starnbergersee. Both belonged to Klaus Fobke, who was the son of Hermann Fobke. The elder Fobke had been one of the original members of the Führer's first bodyguard, the Stosstrupp Adolf Hitler, and like so many of Hitler's old comrades had been rewarded for his loyalty by being given a high party position – in this case, Gauleiter of Pomerania. Located southwest of Munich, the Reichsschule was originally founded by Ernst Röhm as an SA establishment. After the 'Night of the Long Knives', it gained new patrons in Franz Xavier Schwarz, Rudolf Hess and later Martin Bormann. At first part of the Adolf Hitler Schule system, it became the only school controlled by the Party leadership, and its headmaster was unique in reporting direct to the Führer.

Right: A forage or overseas cap belonging to a member of an Ordensburg, together with a pair of epaulettes. This example is stamped inside showing it to have been issued at Vogelsang in the Eifel Mountains. Vogelsang had the world's largest gymnasium when it was built, and it was a facility which saw a lot of use – the curriculum was much stronger on physical tasks than it was on classroom skills. The original plan was for promising young Party members to be sent to an Ordensburg in their mid-20s, after passing through the Adolf Hitler Schule, Reich Labour Service, the Wehrmacht and two or three years as a full-time Party official. Discipline was severe – one of the most feared punishments was fasting, which proved incredibly hard on bodies already being stressed to their physical limits.

Right: A forage cap and epaulettes worn by a student at one of the Nationalpolitische Erziehungsanstalten – National Political Educational Institutions or 'Napolas' for short. The Napolas were boarding schools modelled on Prussian cadet academies, but which were totally Nazi in their outlook. Their curriculum was the same as more conventional schools, though with National Socialist studies replacing religion and with a very strong emphasis on sport. Selection was based more on HJ membership, physical skills, 'Aryan' ancestry and acceptable parents than on any academic talent. It is not surprising that when the Napolas came under the control of SS Gruppenführer August Heissmeyer in 1936, he noted that academic standards were lower than in German grammar schools.

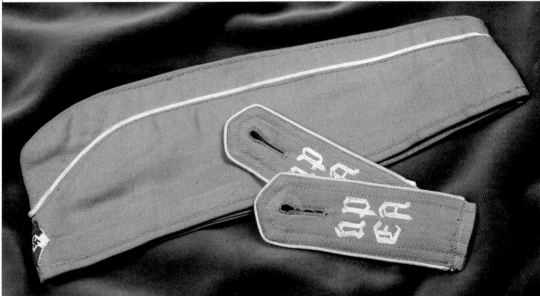

Right: Forage cap and epaulettes worn by a student at one of the Adolf Hitler Schule. Established by Robert Ley and funded until 1941 by the German Labour Front, the Adolf Hitler Schools operated in competition with the Napolas, though with even less emphasis on academic achievement. Potential students were pre-selected in their second year in the Jungfolk of the Hitler Youth, based mainly on their appearance and their leadership qualities. Classes were known as squads, which competed against each other. Teachers were drawn from the HJ leadership and from the Ordensburgen. According to August Heissmeyer, "The knowledge pupils can acquire at Adolf Hitler Schools is in every respect inferior to that provided by more conventional upper schools". In 1939 the curriculum was changed, with more emphasis on academic work.

Joseph Goebbels announces the Anschluss to the Nazi leadership in March 1938, surrounded on all sides by the Swastika. The Nazis hijacked the ancient Sanskrit symbol of good luck, giving the 'hooked cross' a very different meaning.

THE SWASTIKA

THE BLACK, WHITE and red Swastika banner snapping in the wind is the most emotive and easily recognised emblem of Hitler's Third Reich. In war, the Swastika became the symbol of Nazi domination, flying over public and government buildings in six European capitals.

Originally a purely Nazi Party emblem, the red flag with a Swastika within a white disk became an ensign when Hitler came to power in 1933, flying from merchant ships and serving as an identification symbol on

the tail of civil aircraft. In 1935 it was officially declared the German National Flag.

At pre-war political meetings, especially the massive gatherings at Nuremberg, huge Swastika banners attached to buildings or scaffolding served as a backdrop for everything from military parades through torchlit rallies to the Führer's speeches.

RED, WHITE AND BLACK

The Swastika incorporated the red, white and black national colours which were first adopted for the national cockade in 1897

as the symbol of the German Empire. In its earliest form the Swastika was worn as an armband on both civilian clothes or as part of a political uniform. Later, armbands became a uniform item in their own right.

One flag in particular had a special place in Nazi mythology. The *Blutfahne* or 'Blood Banner' was so called from allegedly having been drenched in the blood of the 16 Nazi 'martyrs' killed during the abortive 1923 Beer Hall Putsch in Munich. At the yearly Nuremberg rallies Hitler consecrated new party colours

by touching them with one hand while his other held the bullet-tattered *Blutfahne*.

At the 1933 gathering – the first since the Nazis gained power – the audience listened in silence as the SA leader Ernst Roehm read a long list of Nazi martyrs. He could not have known that he would be dead a year later, as at Hitler's orders the SS eliminated the top SA leadership. Those fellow followers of the Swastika were wiped out in the June 1934 'Night of the Long Knives'.

The *Reichskriegsflagge* or Reich War Flag combined the

Above: The NSDAP membership badge was instituted in 1920, its design being finalised about a decade later. Badges usually came in two sizes, the larger being worn on uniform breast pockets and the smaller worn in the lapel. More than 12 million were manufactured.

Left: The embroidered arm band of a senior Nazi Party official has the swastika edged in gold bullion. Such ostentatious display led to the 'Golden Pheasant' nickname being applied to such men.

Below: The 'Deutschland Erwache' Feldzeichen or standard was probably the most important of all Nazi party symbols in the rise of National Socialism. First introduced in January 1923, it was certainly the most numerous symbol during the Reichsparteitage which were celebrated at the beginning of September each year.

Above: A group of items relating to the SA Sports organisation, including an armband and SA Sports badges in silver and bronze. They use the most common 'mobile' version of the Swastika, with the symbol tilted by 45 degrees.

Left: The anti-partisan badge, reputedly designed personally by Reichsführer-SS Heinrich Himmler, was one of the few campaign or combat awards to feature the sunwheel or rounded Swastika – though it was used in the divisional insignia of several SS units.

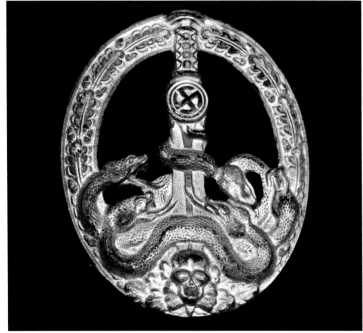

The Swastika was everywhere. It was incorporated into the layout of barrack blocks, trees were planted in Swastika patterns, and at the German Solstice Festival of 21 June 1938 thousands of torch-bearing participants formed a living Swastika in the Berlin Olympic stadium.

UBIQUITOUS SYMBOL

The *Reichsarbeitsdienst* (RAD), the State Labour Organisation in which young men served before they entered the armed forces, incorporated the Swastika into a shovel design, while under the slogan *Blut und Boden* or 'Blood and Soil', the Reich Farmers' organisation intersected the Swastika with a dagger and an ear of corn.

With the outbreak of war, the Swastika became a useful air identification panel. It was carried on the tailplane of combat aircraft, though without the bright red and white colours of the pre-war flag. In its original form it was useful, however, as it enabled Luftwaffe pilots to distinguish between fast-moving German armoured vehicles from the enemy as they advanced through France, Greece, Russia and North Africa. It was attached to the bonnet of wheeled vehicles and the rear decking of tanks.

Despite its modern association with the Nazis, the Swastika is far more ancient than Germany itself. Known as the *hakenkreuz* (hooked cross) or 'fylfot', it is defined in heraldic terms as "a cross of equal arms with rectangular continuations all clockwise or all counter clockwise".

It takes its most common name from the Sanskrit words *su* meaning 'well' and *asti* meaning 'being'. Swastikas can

Swastika with the Prussian Iron Cross, which had been instituted by Kaiser Friedrich Wilhelm in 1813. It was the official ensign of the German armed forces and was flown from warships, over barracks and at formal ceremonies.

The flag was introduced in November 1935 and consisted of a red rectangle with a

Swastika (its arms edged with a narrow black and white border) within a white disk surrounded by a black border off-centre, closer to the mast. The disk was at the centre of a cross with arms made up of four white and three black bars running to the borders of the flag. In the canton (top left hand corner) was an Iron Cross.

Above: In the 1930s, before Germany's military conquest of Europe, there were numerous Anglo-German and German-American voluntary organisations. They existed to promote German relations with the English-speaking world, and members wore lapel badges like these.

Right: The badge of the Deutsche Jägerschaft, or German Huntsman's Association. Titular head of the organisation, the Reichsjägermeister, was one of the most enthusiastic hunters in Germany, whose particular passion was wild boar. His name was Hermann Goering.

Below: Naturally, Swastikas in one form or another adorned the many newspapers and magazines published by the various branches of the Nazi Party. These issues are of the paper produced by the Hitler Youth.

be found in 4th Century BC ceramics from Iran and appeared later in Troy, Greece, Tibet and Japan. In primitive cultures it has been used as a charm against the 'evil eye', while North American Indians often used the Swastika in their bead work designs. In India it was employed to denote the movement of the sun – indeed, pre-war editions of Rudyard Kipling's books set in India usually featured the Swastika on the spine or the cover.

'ARYAN' ORIGINS

In 19th Century Europe the racial and political ideas which were to shape much of the character of Nazi Germany were focused around the confusion between the Indo-European group of languages and the so-called Indo-European race. Late in the century Friedrich Max Muller, an Anglo-German philologist, used the word 'Aryan' to designate the Indo-European language group. He stated very plainly that he was talking about language, and that language and race were two very different things.

Unwittingly Muller had given German racialists a word and a concept on which to hang their bigotry. 'Aryan' came to mean

nobility of blood, incomparable beauty of form and mind, and a superior breed.

Swastika was a Sanskrit word, Sanskrit being the oldest of the Indo-European languages, and thereby acquired its 'Aryan' racial associations. It began to be used as a racist symbol in Germany as early as 1910.

In the years of turmoil after the end of World War I, the

right-wing *Freikorps Ehrhardt* painted large white Swastikas on their helmets as a distinguishing mark, and the symbol was picked up by the nascent National Socialists.

One of the by-products of Nazi fascination with the Aryan race was a bizarre form of pseudo-academic research into the runes and symbols used by ancient Norse tribes of northern

Europe. Many of these would be adopted as insignia for Waffen-SS and Nazi Party uniforms and as divisional markings. The 'sun wheel' version of the Swastika, which had curved outer arms, was adopted by the 11th SS *Panzergrenadier Division Nordland*. It was also used in the badge awarded for anti-Partisan operations.

THE IRON CROSS

INSTITUTED IN 1813 by Friederich Wilhelm III of Prussia, the *Eisernes Kreuz* or Iron Cross was the best known and most highly regarded of all German awards for valour.

Awarded only in wartime, the Iron cross was reconstituted by Hitler at the outbreak of World War II. There were four grades: Second Class, First Class, Knight's Cross and Grand Cross, although the sole wearer of the latter was Hermann Goering.

The Iron Cross was awarded for bravery in the face of the enemy, or for actions above and beyond the call of duty. Approximately three million Second Class awards (EKII) were made, though many were presented to German allies or to civilians. Only those who already held the EKII were eligible to receive the First Class medal, or EKI. Precise numbers of recipients are not known, but may have exceeded 500,000.

The *Ritterkreuz* or Knight's Cross of the Iron Cross was intended to bridge the gap between the Iron Cross 1st Class and the *Grosskreuz* or Grand Cross. Awarded for conspicuous heroism or for outstanding command performance, the Knight's cross was much harder to win than the standard medal.

It came in five classes. These were, in ascending order of precedence, the *Ritterkreuz* (7,200 awarded); *Ritterkreuz mit Eichenlaub* or Knight's Cross with Oak Leaves (853 recipients); *Ritterkreuz mit Eichenlaub and Schwerten* or Knight's Cross with Oak Leaves and Swords (150 recipients); *Ritterkreuz mit Eichenlaub, Schwerten und Brillianten* or Knight's Cross with Oak Leaves, Swords and Diamonds (27 recipients); and *Ritterkreuz mit goldenen Eichenlaub, Schwerten und Brillianten* or Knight's Cross with Golden Oak Leaves, Swords and Diamonds. The only recipient of the Golden Oakleaves was the phenomenal Stuka pilot, Hans-Ulrich Rudel.

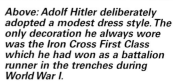

Above: Adolf Hitler deliberately adopted a modest dress style. The only decoration he always wore was the Iron Cross First Class which he had won as a battalion runner in the trenches during World War I.

Left: Field Marshal Erwin Rommel examines the Normandy defences with his chief of staff, Knight's Cross holder Hans Spiedel. Rommel was awarded the Knights Cross in 1940, with the Oakleaves coming in 1941, Swords in January 1942 and Diamonds in March 1943.

Above: A uniform coat once owned by Generalleutnant *Eugen-Heinrich Bleyer, who was awarded the Knight's Cross in December 1941. At the time he was an* Oberstleutnant, *commanding Infantry Regiment 379. Wearers devised a variety of methods to secure their decorations, including hooks, cord and elastic. In the field they would often substitute the original medal for an Iron Cross First Class, the original being stored for safekeeping .*

Right: An Iron Cross First Class of the First World War, bearing the monogram of Kaiser Wilhelm II. Holders of the award from 1914-1918 could wear them on their World War II uniforms, further awards being marked by a bar or Spange *worn on the medal ribbon.*

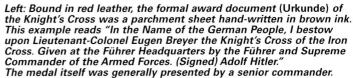

Left: Bound in red leather, the formal award document (Urkunde) of the Knight's Cross was a parchment sheet hand-written in brown ink. This example reads "In the Name of the German People, I bestow upon Lieutenant-Colonel Eugen Breyer the Knight's Cross of the Iron Cross. Given at the Führer Headquarters by the Führer and Supreme Commander of the Armed Forces. (Signed) Adolf Hitler." The medal itself was generally presented by a senior commander.

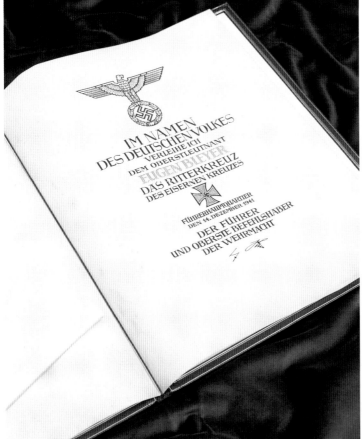

Left: The Iron Cross Second Class was awarded for a single act of bravery, not necessarily in battle. At the award ceremony the medal ribbon was suspended from the second buttonhole of the tunic. The cross itself was only worn on official occasions: in daily use only the ribbon was worn on a ribbon bar or in the buttonhole.

Far left: To be eligible for the Iron Cross First Class, a recipient had to be recommended for the EKII at least three times. The medal was permanently worn on the left breast pocket, though as with all grades of the Iron Cross most used a duplicate of the medal, keeping the original safe.

Right: Der Kriegsorden des Deutschen Kreuzes *or 'War Order of the German Cross' was introduced on 28 September 1941. It was designed to span the significant gap between the EKI and the Ritterkreuz. Awarded in Silver and Gold – the cloth and metal versions of the German Cross in Gold are seen here – a recipient had to perform seven to ten actions over and above that necessary to win the EKI. Approximately 25,000 crosses were awarded, the majority in Gold.*

Below left: In 1940 it became clear that new, higher grades of the Knight's Cross were required. The Oakleaves were awarded for extreme bravery or for a long period of excellence in command. Hitler approved all higher awards personally.

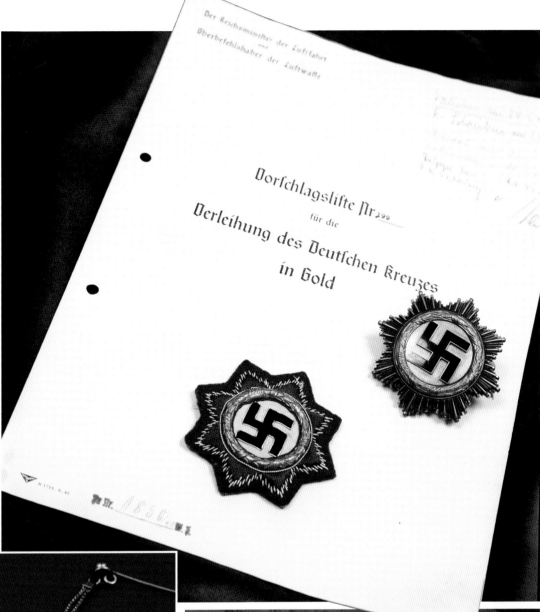

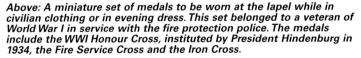

Above: A miniature set of medals to be worn at the lapel while in civilian clothing or in evening dress. This set belonged to a veteran of World War I in service with the fire protection police. The medals include the WWI Honour Cross, instituted by President Hindenburg in 1934, the Fire Service Cross and the Iron Cross.

Right: A parade group of medals which would have been worn by an experienced soldier who had served in both the eastern and western theatres. The group includes the Iron Cross Second Class, the War Merit Cross, the Russian Front Medal and the Westwall medal.

NAZI MEDIA

ADOLF HITLER well knew the value of publicity, even before he won the allegiance of Joseph Goebbels, master of propaganda. Eher Verlag, the central press of the NSDAP, was founded in 1923 under the management of Max Amann, Hitler's sergeant from the trenches.

With the establishment of the Third Reich, Amann became Reich Press Leader, ordered to supervise all matters concerning the German publishing business. According to the 1937

Organisationsbuch der NSDAP, "He is charged with the creation of a press for the German people, which is responsible and answerable to him, and which reflects the life and experiences of the German people's community. The *Reichsleiter* for the Press has the function of issuing regulations necessary to carry out the demands concerning publication policies established in Article 23 of the Party Program and to supervise their execution."

Article 23 of the Party Platform provided that:

Above: Propaganda magazines were a major staple of the Nazi publishing effort once war broke out. Signal, *a highly illustrated magazine, appeared in several European languages, while* Die Wehrmacht *was for consumption by home and uniformed readers.*

(a) all editors and newspaper personnel must be "members of the nation"; (b) non-Germans are prohibited from financial participation in, or influence of, newspapers; (c) the publication of papers "which do not conduce to the national welfare" is prohibited; (d) tendencies in art or literature "of a kind likely to disintegrate our life as a nation" will be prosecuted; and (e) "institutions which militate

against the requirements mentioned above" will be suppressed.

Thus the Reich Press Leader not only controlled Party publishing, but was tasked with bringing the entire German press into line with National Socialist ideology. Amann was given wide powers, which he used to the full. By 1942, he controlled more than 80 percent of all German newspaper publishers.

Above: The Völkischer Beobachter was the central news organ of the NSDAP. Acquired by the Party as early as 1920, it was the most important Nazi propaganda tool through the next decade. From 1922 it was controlled by Max Amann's Eher Verlag, while Dietrich Eckart served as editor until replaced in 1923 by Alfred Rosenberg. Banned after the Putsch, it was reestablished in 1925 with Hitler as publisher. Circulation rose from 4,000 in 1924 to 126,000 in 1932, and after the Nazi assumption of power it became the official German paper of record. By 1938 over 600,000 copies were being printed in Berlin, Munich and Vienna, though readership was much lower.

Right: Staff members of party organs were given distinctive armbands to wear with their party uniforms. Seen here is the metallic badge of a party press photographer, together with the armband of an editor-in-chief.

Above: The NSDAP membership book for a party member working for the Völkischer Beobachter, with stamps showing paid party dues. Party domination of a press which was legally bound to follow the party line did nothing for readability: circulation was dropping at the outbreak of war, and only began to rise when the population began to demand more information during the conflict.

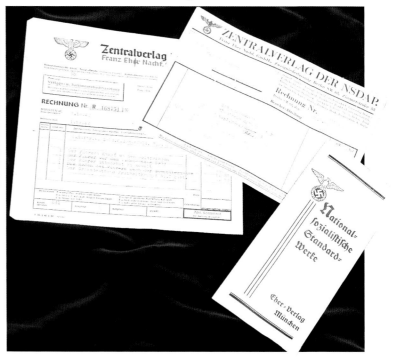

Above: Newspapers have long been a major part of cafe society in Europe, and most such establishments have copies of various publications on wire holders for patrons to read. This was just as true under the Third Reich as it is today, and this example was used to display copies of Der Führer. Der Führer was an illustrated broadsheet published by the NSDAP Gau in Baden, edited by Gauleiter and Reich Governer Robert Wagner.

Right: The Zentralverlag der NSDAP was the name Eher Verlag took for the publishing of official party material. This ranged from the Völkischer Beobachter through party magazines like Das Schwarze Korps produced for the SS to Hitler's autobiography and political platform, Mein Kampf. Seen here are a pair of Zentralverlag invoices, together with a publicity brochure for Standarte GmbH, the Eher company responsible for publishing local Gau-level newspapers.

Above: Photograph books about the Führer, illustrated and written by his personal photographer. Heinrich Hoffmann, an old party comrade, was the only person officially allowed to photograph Hitler, and his books presented his master in the best possible light. Their popularity contributed to the immense wealth Hoffmann amassed during the Third Reich.

Left: Also immensely popular, but for very much darker reasons, were the books produced by Julius Streicher's Stürmerverlag. Der Giftpilz, (The Toadstool) and 'Don't trust a fox in the field – Don't trust a Jew on his oath' were violently ant-Semitic comic books aimed particularly at young children. Pages were typically entitled 'How Jewish traders cheat', 'Money is the god of all Jews', and 'How the peasant was swindled out of his farm'.

FOREIGN NAZIS

Mussolini was the role model for pre-war Fascist leaders: few who followed the Nazi model achieved any political success before the war.

Czech Nazis salute the obliteration of the country of Czechoslovakia on 5 April 1939. Slovakia was given 'independence', though in reality it was nothing more than a Nazi puppet state. Bohemia and Moravia became a Reich protectorate under Konstantin von Neurath, with the eager assistance of the Nazi-inspired and funded Sudeten German Party.

T HE FIRST FASCIST political party came into being in 1919 and was followed by an array of imitators. In many ways, Mussolini's fascist movement was the model on which all other right-wing nationalist organisations were based. Authoritarian, anti-communist and anti-democratic movements came to power in Hungary, Austria, Poland, Romania, Spain, Portugal and Argentina as well as in Germany.

Fascists had their greatest following in Catholic countries, or in predominantly Catholic areas of more heterogeneous states; Catholicism fostered the centralist and hierarchical state of mind under which such regimes prospered.

GERMAN-STYLE NAZIS

The success of Hitler and the Nazis in the 1930s inspired a number of Fascist parties on the German model. Those in states with a democratic, secular tradition remained fringe movements. Sir Oswald Moseley's Blackshirts, the British Union of Fascists, held some spectacular meetings on the

Above: The Sudeten German Home Front was founded in October 1933 by Konrad Henlein. It was renamed the Sudetendeutsche Partei – Sudeten German Party or SdP – in 1935. By this time it was an overtly Nazi organisation, largely funded from Berlin. The membership book, armband and lapel badges seen here date from after the change.

Right: Norway's Nasjonal Samling or National Assembly was a Fascist splinter party headed by former army officer Vidkun Quisling. Unlike the Sudeten Nazis, Quisling had little popular support, and he was little more than a German figurehead. This did not stop him issuing a whole set of awards and insignia: these are a labour collar patch, a ski-cap badge and a service medal.

Reichsparteitag model, and fought running street battles with socialists and Communists in London's East End. But their right-wing, anti-semitic message was not popular, and these extremists stood no chance of achieving power. The same could be said of Fritz Kuhn's German-American *Bund*.

Similar fringe parties were formed in Belgium, where Leon Degrelle's Catholic Rexist movement had some small success, but Vidkun Quisling's *Nasjonal Samling* in Norway and Anton Mussert's *National-Socialistische Beweging* enjoyed little popular support. Neither had a hope of achieving any power until their countries were occupied by the Germans in 1940. Even then they remained totally under the thumb of their German overlords.

Only in Austria and the Sudetenland did German-style Fascism really take hold. The Austrian NSDAP mounted an unsuccessful putsch in 1934 before engineering the *Anschluss* four years later, and Konrad Henlein's 'Sudeten German Party' were instrumental in forging the dismemberment of Czechoslovakia.

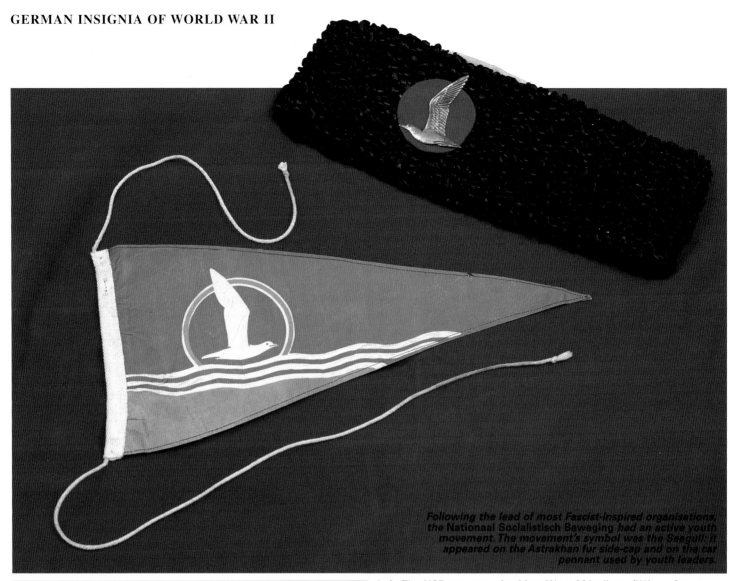

Following the lead of most Fascist-inspired organisations, the Nationaal Socialistisch Beweging had an active youth movement. The movement's symbol was the Seagull: it appeared on the Astrakhan fur side-cap and on the car pennant used by youth leaders.

Left: The NSB was organised into Weer Afdeeligen (WA, or Storm Detachments) which combined to make up a Vendel or Division. The NSB made extensive use of the traditional Dutch colour of orange in place of the Nazi red, and many of their badges and insignia carried the 'Wolfshook' rune. The rank badge, epaulette, cap badge and cuff title seen here were worn by a member of the Dietschland Vendel.

Right: An NSB peaked visor cap with triangular 'Wolfshook' insignia and flaming grenade badge. The 'Wolfshook' rune derives from the ancient Germanic Wolfsangel, which was supposed to be a magical symbol able to of frighten wolves. The symbol was also used by SS Division Das Reich and by late-war 'Werewolf' units.

Holland's home-grown Nazis

Anton Mussert founded the *Nationaal Socialistiche Beweging* in 1931 whilst he was a middle-level civil servant. Initially influenced by the Italian Fascists, the movement evolved into a Nazi-style Party. Anti-Semitic and anti-Communist in nature, the NSB platform also included a desire to unite the Netherlands and Dutch-speaking Flanders. The new country was to be called Dietschland.

BRIEF POPULARITY

In 1933, Mussert could attract less than 600 people to a meeting in Utrecht, where the Party was based. A year later, some 25,000 turned out. Mussert's growing political profile was not popular with his employers, and he was fired from his government job for "pernicious political activity and treachery to the state."

The Party reached a peak of popularity in the 1935 elections, polling over 300,000 votes, but most of these gains were lost in the 1937 elections. Appointed assistant to *Reichskommissar* Artur Seyss-Inquart after the German occupation, Mussert and his Party's active collaboration with the Nazis saw him tried for treason after the war. The Party was banned, and Mussert was condemned to die. He was hanged in May 1946.

Above: Anton Adrian Mussert was the founder and leader of the Dutch National Socialist Movement. Born in 1894, he trained as a hydraulic engineer, and after World War I worked as a civil servant with the Department of Dykes, Roads, Bridges and Canals. He was notably anti-Semitic: the headline on this poster reads "No Jews!"

Like in common with all fascist leaders, Mussert attempted to establish a personality cult. Very few of the images used in publicity material such as this calendar gave any clue that the Leider or "Leader" was less than five feet tall. The arm badge depicted shows the NSB's emblem: the divided red and black triangle symbolises "Blood and Soil" (a belief the NSB shared with the Nazis), while the central shield depicts the national lion on the Dutch colours of orange-white-blue.

REICH SECURITY

Although the SS Security Service was founded by Heinrich Himmler long before the Nazis came to power, Reinhard Heydrich was the driving force behind the growth of the organisation and the fearsome reputation it acquired under the Third Reich.

Germany under the Nazis was a police state. A widespread security apparatus was designed to hunt down enemies of that state.

THE TANGLED WEB which was the organisation of the security services under the Third Reich was not made any clearer by the fact that often members of one body, such as the Gestapo, would wear the uniform of another body, such as the SD, under varying circumstances.

As the SD expanded, its work overlapped with that of the Gestapo. Friction ensued as the Party's secret police and the state secret police hunted down the same people. However, party and state security forces were soon indistinguishable. On 23 June 1938 it was decreed that all Gestapo and Kripo (*Kriminalpolizei*, or plain-clothed detectives) must enroll in the SS.

On 29 September 1939, as the Polish campaign drew to a close, all of Germany's plain-clothes security services were placed under Heydrich's control. The Gestapo and Kripo, known collectively as the SIPO (*Sicherheitspolizei* – security police) were brought together with the SD into a single administration, the all-embracing *Reichsicherheitshauptamt* (RSHA – Reich Central Security Office).

An example of an SD NCO's peaked visor cap and weapons belt. The belt buckle carries the standard SS motto "Mein Ehre Heisst Treue" – My Honour is Loyalty – but the toxic green Waffenfarbe or arm-of service piping was unique to the security services. During the war this was changed to white, as worn by the rest of the SS.

Although Nazi security agents normally wore plain clothes, outside Germany itself this might have caused problems. As a result, security personnel were issued with SD uniforms – whether or not they were members of the SD, the SS, or even the Nazi Party.

The uniform was a grey regulation *Allgemeine-SS* 1938 pattern, with SS rank insignia on the left collar patch and a blank right collar patch. The SD sleeve diamond had first been introduced with the establishment of the old *SD-Hauptamt* in Berlin's Wilhelmstrasse after the seizure of power.

In the 1930s the *SD-Hauptamt* was divided into three main *Ämter* or offices – *Amt I* 'Organisation', *Amt II*

'Combatting Opposition', and *Amt III* 'Foreign Countries'. The three *Ämter* served as a kind of 'General Staff' of intelligence activities, controlling seven *Oberabschnitte* or sections. Each *Oberabschnitt* had two or three *Unterabschnitte*, which in turn coordinated the *SD-Aussenstellen* or 'out-stations' covering individual rural districts or towns.

The *Sicherheitsdienst* was mainly a collator of information provided by other bodies such as the Gestapo, and there were SD offices all over Germany. However, while the SD might have as many as 50,000 informants on its books at one time, its full-time staff was only about 3,000 in the late 1930s.

Below: Almost as much of a symbol of the secret police as the Gestapo leather coat, the Walther PP or Polizei Pistole was standard issue to members of the SD. First appearing in 1929, the PP was an excellent handgun. It was also manufactured in kurz or shortened form as the PPK, specifically designed for concealed carriage by plain-clothes men.

An armband carrying the phrase "In the service of the security police." The armband was worn by civilian auxiliaries working temporarily with the Sicherheitspolizei and the SD late in the war. This example dates from August 1944.

Below: As with most Nazi organisations, the Security Police and the Security Service of the SS had their own newspaper. Although originally a purely party organisation, the SD gradually became more and more interlinked with the Sicherheitspolizei (which incorporated the Kriminalpolizei, the Security Police and the Gestapo. Eventually, in 1939, the organisations became one.

Above: A set of non-commissioned officer insignia worn by a member of the Schutzmannschaft. 'Schumas' were foreign, non-German auxiliaries brought in to assist the SD and the security police in the Eastern territories. Their motto, as seen on the arm badge above, was 'Treue, Tapfer, Gehorsam', or 'Loyal, Valiant and Obedient'.

SS Intelligence Service

SD-Abschnitte
Berlin
Breslau
Danzig
Dresden
Düsseldorf
Hamburg
Karlsruhe
Kattowitz
Königsberg
München
Nürnberg
Posen
Prag (Prague)
Reichenberg
Stettin
Stuttgart
Wien (Vienna)

SD-Unterabschnitte
Bayreuth
Braunschweig (Brunswick)
Bremen
Dessau
Dortmund
Frankfurt / Main
Graz
Halle / Saale
Innsbruck
Kassel
Kiel
Klagenfurt
Koblenz
Köln (Cologne)
Linz / Donau
Litzmannstadt
Münster / Westfalen
Saarbrücken
Schwerin / Mecklenburg
Weimar
Zichenau

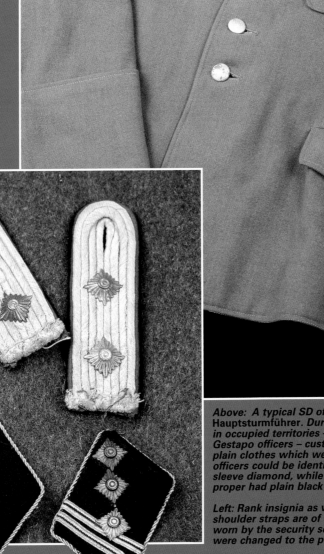

Above: A typical SD officer's tunic as worn by an SD-Hauptsturmführer. During the war, Security Police personnel working in occupied territories – the detectives of the Kriminalpolizei and Gestapo officers – customarily wore SD uniforms rather than the plain clothes which were normal in Greater Germany. Gestapo officers could be identified by the silver border worn around the SD sleeve diamond, while the diamonds worn by members of the SD proper had plain black edges.

Left: Rank insignia as worn by an Hauptsturmführer in the SD. The shoulder straps are of standard SS-pattern, with the green piping worn by the security services. After 1942, epaulettes on SD uniforms were changed to the police pattern in black and silver.

CIVILIANS IN UNIFORM

At the height of Hitler's rule, it seemed as though every German was in uniform.

Germany has long been a nation of uniforms, so when the paramilitary SA formations were banned from wearing their brown shirts it hit the Nazi Party hard. However, when they came to power they immediately Nazified the uniforms worn by civil organisations.

THE ITALIANS might have had the edge when it came to style, but the Nazis were the masters of the art of using uniforms to define a person's place in society. All countries use uniforms and insignia to symbolise differences in rank or influence, but the Germans spread the concept beyond military and political organisations to most civilian bodies as well. Uniforms were also a psychologically important tool to the Nazis: the use of National Socialist symbols on the insignia, used by all state and local bodies, was indicative of the Party's octopus-like hold on every aspect of public life.

SOME LIKE IT GREY

Most people will be familiar with the military regalia, rank badges and decorations of the Wehrmacht and the Waffen-SS, and items worn by Nazi organisations such as the SA, the Hitler Youth and the Police are much sought after by collectors of militaria, but these were simply the tip of the iceberg. There were at least sixty-four distinct uniformed organisations, in Hitler's Germany, ranging from nationwide bodies such as the *Reichsarbeitsdienst* and the National Railway Service through volunteer organisations such as the German Red Cross down to specialised groupings

Above: An officer's peaked cap of the Technische Nothilfe – *the Technical Emergency Service, or TeNo. Formed in 1919 as a strike-breaking organisation of ex-military engineers tasked with keeping essential services going, it evolved into a body of experts who could give advice in major civil emergencies.*

Under the Nazis the TeNo was absorbed into the police, and during the war became closely associated with the Waffen-SS, being used for engineering work behind the front lines. Seen here are a unit right-hand collar patch, a rank left-hand collar patch worn by NCOs, a cuff-title and a triangular cloth cap badge.

such as the *Deutschen Falkenorden* and the *Deutscher Jägerschaft* – respectively responsible for falconry and hunting – and the National Stud Farms in East and West Prussia, officials of which had their own unique rank insignia.

Below: An officer's peaked visor cap of the Deutsches Rotes Kreuz – the German Red Cross or DRK. Although it was the German branch of the International League of the Red Cross, which had been founded in 1869, it had come into the Nazi orbit in 1939, when its organisation was centralised under the personal patronage of Adolf Hitler.

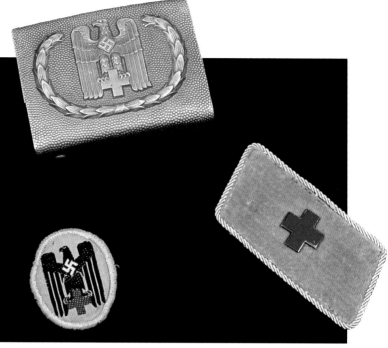

Above: A set of DRK insignia, comprising a belt buckle worn by volunteers and lower ranks, a cloth cap badge, and the silver-piped collar patch which was worn by all ranks up to DRK-Generalführer.

Below: In 1937, the nationalised but independently-run Deutsche Reichsbahn became a government agency. It was the largest enterprise in Germany, and one of the largest employers. The wartime insignia depicted below include an armband worn by helpers and officials, an arm badge and cuffband worn by a military liaison official in Brussels, and a collar patch introduced in 1942 for middle-ranking officials.

Above: An NSLB lapel button. The NS Lehrerbund, or National Socialist Teachers League, was the party organisation tasked with persuading Germany's educators to follow the Party line.

Right: A tunic worn by an Oberzollinspekteur of the Land Customs Service, working in administration. The letters RFV on the shoulder strap stand for Reichsfinanzverwaltung, or National Finance Administration. On the breast pocket are the Iron Cross First Class and the SA Sports Badge in Bronze.

Below: German postal, telegraph and telecommunications services were controlled by the Deutsche Reichspost. Officials wore blue tunics and caps, with orange piping and collar patches.

PARTY MEMBERS

Without military decorations of his own, Reichsführer-SS Heinrich Himmler had to make do with Party awards to adorn his uniform. He is seen here wearing an SA Bronze Sports badge and the Golden Party Badge on his left breast pocket. The ribbon in the buttonhole of the right pocket is the Blood Order, awarded to those who took part in the 1923 Beer Hall Putsch.

To be a Nazi Party member was a definite advantage, career-wise, in the early years of Hitler's rule.

NSDAP PARTY membership was not always something to be trumpeted in Nazi Germany, particularly after the war turned against the Reich. People needed a scapegoat and the inefficiency and corruption of the Party State gave them an easy target of hatred. But during the years of Hitler's ascendancy, membership of the Party was often the only route to success. Ambitious men who had not already joined the movement were quick to take the plunge. Membership grew from less than a million in 1933 to nearly three million in 1935. By 1945, there were over eight and a half million paid-up members of the NSDAP.

MEMBERSHIP DISPLAY

Party officials were easy to recognise because they wore the brown uniform and extensive decoration which led to their nickname of 'Golden Pheasants'. SA and SS men also wore distinctive uniforms. However, the bulk of the membership of the Party were ordinary citizens, who were usuallly identified by their party membership badges or the lapel pins indicating that they belonged to one of the many specialist party organisations, or state bodies over which the party had control.

Introduced in 1920 and

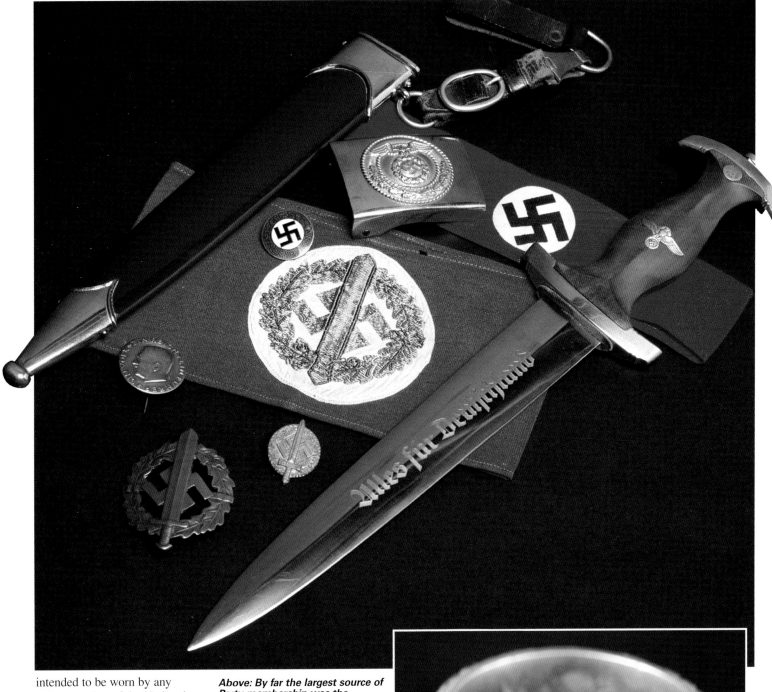

intended to be worn by any active member of the National Socialist German Worker's Party, the Party Badge was a simple swastika with a red enamelled surround. It was manufactured in huge numbers, at least ten million having been awarded before the end of World War II.

The Party membership badge was generally worn in addition to any other decorations. For civilians, or for military personnel in civilian dress, these normally took the form of lapel pins or buttonholes.

Above: By far the largest source of Party membership was the NSDAP's paramilitary arm, the Sturm Abteilung, or SA. Most of the regalia and equipment carried was specific to the SA – seen here are the dagger, rally armband, sports armband and badges – but the small party membership badge was worn with honour.

Right: One symbol which could only be worn by Party members – indeed, which could only be worn by members of the SS, and only those in good standing with the Reichsführer-SS, was the Death's Head ring. In the personal gift of Heinrich Himmler, it recognised the wearer's devotion to duty and loyalty to the Führer.

GOLDEN PARTY BADGE

Above: Although the Golden Party Badge was intended for the original members of the Nazi Party, Hitler later widened its scope by awarding it to "those who have particularly distinguished themselves in the National Socialist Movement, and who have helped in the attainment of its goals." Later party members who were awarded the badge included Albert Speer and Hitler's military 'Yes-man', Wilhelm Keitel.

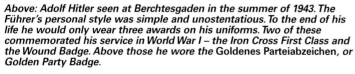

Above: Adolf Hitler seen at Berchtesgaden in the summer of 1943. The Führer's personal style was simple and unostentatious. To the end of his life he would only wear three awards on his uniforms. Two of these commemorated his service in World War I – the Iron Cross First Class and the Wound Badge. Above those he wore the Goldenes Parteiabzeichen, or Golden Party Badge.

Right: Julius Streicher talks with Joachim von Ribbentrop. Streicher, who was Gauleiter of Franconia, publisher of der Stürmer, and the NSDAP's arch-anti-semite, was a wearer of the Gold Party Badge. Initially, the badge could only be worn by the first 100,000 members of the NSDAP, and it became a symbol of the Nazi 'Old Guard'.

Above: Founded by the Air Ministry in 1933, the Reichsluftschütz Bund (RLB, or Reich Air Defence League) was a voluntary civil defence organisation taken over by the NSDAP in 1944.

Below: Lapel badges of the Reichsnährstand or Reich Food Estate. This organisation was responsible for all National Socialist agricultural policy. Leader Walther Darré, came up with the catchy slogan Blut und Boden – 'Bread and Blood'.

Above: Lapel badges worn by members of the Reichs Arbeitsdienst, or Reich Labour Service. The Nazis were great believers in the notion that all citizens had an obligation to work for the state. The badge of the RAD included ears of wheat symbolising work on the land, and a spade which represented manual labour.

Right: The Party did its best to organise every worker in Germany, from the largest industries to the smallest one-man operation. This badge was worn by the Reichsbund Deutscher Kleingartner – the National League of German Allotment Growers.

Below: Lapel badges worn by members and participants in Kraft durch Freude or 'Strength through Joy.' The massive leisure organisation was one of the key routes used by the NSDAP in spreading the National Socialist message through the general populace.

The Reich Culture Chamber or Reichs-kulturkammer controlled all artistic and creative life in Hitler's Germany. Without the approval of the Chamber no artist, theatrical performer, writer or broadcaster could do any work.

Index